D0441670

The Authority of the Bible

The Authority
of the Bible

Donald G. Miller

WILLIAM B. EERDMANS PUBLISHING COMPANY
Grand Rapids, Michigan

To the
PASTOR
and
MEMBERS OF THE CONGREGATION
of the
FIRST PRESBYTERIAN CHURCH
of
RICHMOND, VIRGINIA

Preface

The central conviction of this volume was voiced by John Calvin in his "First Sermon on Pentecost" when he said that "men have not invented what is contained in the Old and New Testaments," but that "God is the real author" of their teaching.

The study of the Bible has come a long way since Calvin's day. We are better able to distinguish God's Word from the words of men through which it comes. But when the Bible is reduced to mere ancient literature, an anthology of the thoughts of men long gone, with no authoritative and unchanging truth of which "God is the real author," the church is left with no word "from above" by which to nourish her life or to guide her destiny. Whether this slight volume makes any contribution to the solution of the problem it raises the reader must judge for himself. There can be little doubt that the issue is an important one.

I am fully aware of the book's limitations. It is incomplete; space forbade a total look at a problem so vast and complex. It is not a "scholarly" but a "popular" study, designed to be read by laymen and pastors too busy to delve into the intricacies of the subject. It is not innovative, but is rather an effort in recovery. "Old stuff" may be the major criticism of some reviewers, with too few contemporary authors consulted. The writer is prepared to accept this criticism. C. S. Lewis spoke of a "chronological snobbery" which assumes that what is current is true and what is out of date is false. It may be that creditable writers of an earlier time have *more* to say to us than contemporary writers, just because they are saying what is no longer heard, but should be.

The church needs, for herself and for the world, an authoritative (not an authoritarian!) word. This word can never be her own. It comes *to* her—from God. God "spoke" through the prophets and finally through His Son. The record of this speaking is in the Bible. If we are to hear, we must listen *there,* where He has chosen to speak. It is hoped that this volume may encourage some to attune their ears afresh to listen for the voice of the living God through the ancient Book.

Gratitude is due, and heartily given, to the pastor, Dr. James A. Jones III, and the members of the congregation of the First Presbyterian Church of Richmond, Virginia, who listened so attentively and responded so graciously when these chapters were first spoken as the Carson Memorial Lectures in May, 1971; and to Mrs. Tom E. Benton, whose patience and skill in typing the manuscript were surpassing.

—D.G.M.

Contents

Chapter One

The Problem of Biblical Authority

In the seventeenth century, John Bunyan, author of *Pilgrim's Progress,* shows us how bound to the authority of the Bible he was. He writes:

> But one day, as I was passing in the field . . . with some dashes on my Conscience, fearing lest yet all was not right, suddenly this sentence fell upon my soul, *Thy righteousness is in Heaven;* and methought withal, I saw, with the Eyes of my Soul, Jesus Christ at God's Right Hand. . . . Now did my Chains fall off my Legs indeed; I was loosed from my Afflictions and Irons; . . . now went I also home rejoicing, for the Grace and Love of God. So when I came home, I looked to see if I could find that sentence, *Thy Righteousness is in Heaven,* but could not find such a saying; wherefore my Heart began to sink again. . . .[1]

Bunyan was so trustful of the authority of the Scriptures that if the words that had brought release and hope to him were not really there, he could not trust his emotional experience of freedom from guilt. Although he never found the particular wording he sought, he ultimately found a resting place for his soul on other biblical passages which contained the same truth. For Bunyan, no word outside the Bible could be authoritative in the realm of the soul's struggle.

Contrast this with two recent instances. A minister friend of mine, impressed by Neil Armstrong's walk on the moon, felt that such a significant moment should not go unnoticed in the pulpit. Shunning the bizarre and the sensational, he prepared a sermon for the following Sunday on the first chapter of Colossians, where Jesus is depicted as the agent of creation, both of things visible and invisible, and as the One who holds the universe together, the One who is preeminent in the whole cosmos. The next Tuesday morning he received a letter from one of the officers of his church, upbraiding him for his effort and saying: "What did those ancient rustics know about modern life?" In other words, the Bible is irrelevant to a scientific age.

Many who share this view would, however, reserve a place for the authority of Jesus in the realm of the inner life. They feel that although Jesus is irrelevant to any discussion of scientific achievements, He did have a profound understanding of man and his relation to God, and His word in these areas is permanently relevant. But this view too is gone for many, even in the church. Recently I was confronted by a young minister following a worship service I had led at a minister's conference. After an interchange of a few minutes, I asked him if he thought I had misinterpreted the passage in Matthew on which I had spoken. He replied: "Oh, no, I think Matthew thought what you proposed; in fact, I think that even Jesus thought that. But Jesus had never read Reinhold Niebuhr!" I asked him if he was serious. When he answered in the affirmative, I replied: "Well, then, our conversation is at an end. Let me suggest to you one thing, however. Don't let Reinhold Niebuhr hear you say that!" For such as these, neither Jesus nor the apostles have any valid word for the perplexing problems of our time or the struggles that vex our inner lives.

Much of this sort of thing is not very profound. It reflects what H. Scott Holland describes as an intellectual adolescence, which carries us back to old days of happy boyish confidence, when we swung along in the flood of our first philosophic raptures, gaily shocking our sisters in the Vacation, and bringing a pained surprise into the sweet, patient face of our mother. It was all so sure—and we were so pleased with large sweeping phrases—and there was no time to stop and make the necessary qualifications; we disposed of things with such a grand air of freedom. We saw no difficulties—we came to no check—for, indeed, before the objections had got time to show themselves, we were off and away to something else. That is a mood familiar to us all.[2]

But granted that the views expressed above may be frequently accounted for by the fact that today "the unorthodox in religion has a certain adventitious glamour about it,"[3] they likely are more typical than we may suppose, if for no other reason than that most men today do not read, study, or consult the Bible on matters of behavior or values. J. R. Green's description of seventeenth-century England (which could also be applied to America in its early days)—that the Bible was "the one book which was familiar to every Englishman"[4]—has long been outdated. A New York clergyman some time back said that he was rapidly gaining a reputation for wide reading and erudition simply by quoting the Bible!

The alleged freedom with which many approach the authority of the Bible is not really freedom from authority but a bondage to other unacknowledged, or perhaps unconscious, authorities. F. J. A. Hort once remarked that much Christian criticism "is merely the tool for reaching a result not itself believed on that ground but on the ground of speculative postulates; while such postulates though they may be suggested by a multitude of facts . . . yet draw their strength rather from the temporary feeling of an age, in other words from a masked authority or tradition."[5] P. T. Forsyth seconded this when he said,

> What has often passed as the new theology is no more, some-
> times, than a theology of fatigue, or a theology of the press, or
> a theology of views, or a theology of revolt. Or it is an
> accommodation theology, a theology accommodated only to
> the actual interests of the cultured hour. The effort made is to
> substitute for the old faith something more human in its
> origin, more humane in its temper . . . something more genial
> and more rational and more shallow . . . which is mainly hu-
> man nature re-edited and bowdlerized.[6]

Sometimes, too, the veiled authority which dictates our
response to Scripture is outright unbelief. Hence, the
vaunted emancipation, so precious to many in our generation, may be but a masked slavery, the exchange of "the
master light of all our seeing" for an unburnished reflector
of the flickering lights of this present confused and tragic
hour.

The problem of biblical authority, of course, is partly
indicative of a much wider problem—the problem of *any*
authority. There is a history behind this. The Renaissance
and the Reformation began together and were closely
related. "Erasmus laid the egg which Luther hatched."[7]
Erasmus and Luther soon parted company, however, for
their motivating principle differed. The Renaissance was
humanistic. The Reformation, though it used humanistic
tools to further its ends, was evangelical and religious.
Although Erasmus himself was no revolutionary, his principles led to revolution. Those of Luther, who was more by
nature a revolutionary than Erasmus, led not to revolution
but to religious reformation. The thought of Erasmus
produced the French Revolution; that of Luther the Protestant Church. The thought of Erasmus fostered "a proud
feeling of man's self-sufficiency and his independence of
God"; the thought of Luther kindled "a deep sense of
man's insufficiency and of his dependence upon God."[8]

The Western world has developed more along the lines
of the Renaissance than of the Reformation. Both the
American Revolution and the French Revolution, though

numbering men of evangelical religious faith among their participants, were in principle expressions at best of Deism, or at worst Atheism. Voltaire and Rousseau—whose writings, if they did not "cause" the French Revolution, at least served as vehicles for expressing it[9]—and Jefferson and Franklin, who were formative minds in the American experiment, were not evangelical Christians. Erasmus would likely be at home in a modern university, with its humanistic trends. Luther would not. He wrote that the universities in his day were largely "places for the training of youth in the fashions of Greek culture," where "loose living is practiced, where little is taught of the Holy Scriptures and Christian faith."[10]

The tradition of the Renaissance, with man at the center of its thought rather than God, in seeking the goal of liberty for man has tended to define freedom as independence. It has thought of man as an entity in himself, the secret of whose existence is in his own life, or at most in his fellowship with other men. It would hold that if man is created by God, he has been so made that the meaning of his own being is within himself. Personal fellowship with the Creator is not necessary to fullness of life. Man, therefore, "is free so far as he is independent, he is unfree so far as he is dependent."[11] This idea reached perhaps its fullest expression in Fichte, who held that "the self is identical with God, and this self creates the world."[12] Karl Marx phrased it: "Man is free only if he owes his existence to himself."[13] How often echoes of this are heard in our time when we hear people, who may little suspect its source, speak of the self-sufficiency of man, or of man creating his own future.

I have inserted this into the discussion here to indicate that the problem of biblical authority is not an isolated one. It is part and parcel of a total breakdown of authority in modern life, stemming from the full outworking of the Renaissance principle of humanism. It is assumed that if all men are equal, not only in value but in qualities, then

all men are alike. There are no differences in ability,
training, experience, achievement, position, or function in
society. All men are identical. There is "neither superior
nor inferior, greater nor less, better nor worse, stronger nor
weaker."[14] Is it any wonder, then, that we have academic,
political, and social chaos? Everyone is independent of
everyone else. Everyone must be involved in every decision. Everyone is autonomous, everyone is self-governed.
This position, then, makes it questionable whether there
can be any true government. There certainly can be no
genuine community, for community rests not only on
"likeness" between men but on qualities of "unlikeness,"
where because of innate ability, training, skill, or experience some are assigned functions that not all can perform.
Community means "mutual dependence" and "functional
interdependence," which as Emil Brunner points out,

> is based on the principle of supplementation and the structural
> subordination of each individual within a functional unit. . . .
> Now, in this functional unity there is always a subordination
> alongside equal dignity. The one must be above, the other
> below; the one must lead, the other obey. Wherever men have
> to do something together, there must be a hierarchy of com-
> petence, of command; where this is not recognized, the co-
> operative unit falls to pieces.[15]

Shakespeare put it well in *Antony and Cleopatra:*

> *Equality of two domestic powers*
> *Breeds scrupulous faction.*[16]

This is a quite logical outcome of the Renaissance principle. It can be overcome, in my judgment, in one of two
ways. Chaos may be put down by raw power and brute
force (God forbid) or by a return to the Reformation
principle of the nature and dignity of man. Modern events
have taught us, or should have, that "history is not its own
redeemer,"[17] that "man's problems cannot be solved by
man; man's diseases cannot be cured by man; man's sins

cannot be atoned for by man. Nothing that man is, or
thinks, or resolves, or does, avails aught for his deliverance
from sin."[18] In precisely this fact lies the failure of the
Renaissance principle, glorious though it has been in its
achievements during the past four centuries. It has within
it the seeds of its own destruction.

Nowhere has this been delineated more incisively than
by Nicholas Berdyaev in *The End of Our Time*. He writes:

> The Renaissance began with the affirmation of man's creative
> individuality; it has ended with its denial. Man without God is
> no longer man; that is the religious meaning of the internal
> dialectic of modern history, the history of the grandeur and of
> the dissipation of humanist illusions. Interiorly divided and
> drained of his spiritual strength, man becomes the slave of base
> and inhuman influences; his soul is darkened and alien spirits
> take possession of it. The elaboration of the humanist religion
> and the divinization of man and of humanity properly forbode
> the end of humanism. The flowering of the idea of humanity
> was possible only so long as man had a deep belief in and
> consciousness of principles above himself, and was not alto-
> gether cut off from his divine roots. During the Renaissance he
> still had this belief and consciousness and was therefore not
> yet completely separated; throughout modern history the
> European has not totally repudiated his religious basis. It is
> thanks to that alone that the idea of humanity remained
> consistent with the spread of individualism and of creative
> activity. The humanism of Goethe had a religious foundation,
> he kept his faith in God. The man who has lost God gives
> himself up to something formless and inhuman, prostrates
> himself before material necessity. Nowadays there is none of
> that "Renaissential" play and inter-play of human powers
> which gave us Italian painting and Shakespeare and Goethe;
> instead inhuman forces, spirits unchained from the deep, crush
> man and becloud his image, beating upon him like waves from
> every side. It is they, not man, who have been set free. Man
> found his form and his identity under the action of religious
> principles and energies; the confusion in which he is losing
> them cannot be reordered by purely human efforts.[19]

According to the Bible, man is not autonomous. The secret of his existence is not within himself. He is a creature of God's love, who finds his humanity not in himself, nor in other men, but in his relation to God. Therefore "man is a true self or person, and . . . has freedom in so far as he is not in himself or by himself, but in God, *i.e.* in so far as he does not determine himself, but lets himself be determined by God. . . . The more man is sufficient unto himself, the less he is free; and the less he suffices for himself and seeks his life and meaning in God, the freer he is."[20]

The problem of biblical authority, then, is a part of the problem of the authority of *God* over human life. If there is no God, and freedom means full and total human independence, then there is *no* authority; hence, there is no biblical authority. If, however, there is a God, and if He has authority over human life, then the question of the authority of the Bible becomes a live one. The existence of God cannot be rationally proved, although there are many signs that point to its truth. It is rather a basic assumption, an axiom self-evident to many, on which life is built. All that may be said here is that an examination of the history of the race would seem to suggest that the outcomes have been better when men lived on the assumption of the existence of God than when they assumed the opposite. But this, again, is a matter of judgment. Nietzsche and Marx would not agree. We shall proceed here, however, on the assumption that God exists. If that be false, then the whole question of the authority of the Bible is but "stuff and nonsense."

It has been the broad experience of countless thousands through the generations, that when they begin with the assumption of the existence of God, this assumption is confirmed by the actualities of experience. The assumption is usually at first accepted on some authority, be it of parents, Sunday School teacher, minister, or friend. We do not live in a vacuum. Our assumptions usually come from someone else. We do not discover for ourselves that 2 x 2 equals 4. We accept it on the authority of parent or teacher. The assumption, however, is verified for us as we mature and live by it. So it is with belief in God. We are not left without witness. We have the experience of the race, the witness of parents, religious teachers, and the church to instill into us this assumption. But when the assumption is put to the test of life, as the late Archbishop William Temple said, the believer is "brought . . . into ever closer relations with a Being who claims the allegiance of his entire nature—desire and thought, conscience and will. He is delivered, not from, but to, authority, though to authority of a new kind; for the point on which he has reached personal conviction is the existence of a God entitled to exercise authority over him, and of his own consequent obligation to serve and obey that God."[21] The Archbishop points out that there is no conflict here with reason. Just as it is reasonable "for the ignorant man to trust and implicitly to follow the expert" on some subject of worldly wisdom, so "to the devout man it would seem the height of unreason that he should set up his judgment against that of his God."[22] If there is a God, and that God is good, and I may know His loving will, then that will is absolutely authoritative over me in every aspect of life.

What, then, is the nature of this authority? The nature of the authority must be in accord with the nature of the God who wields it. Authority may be coercive, enforced by physical compulsion or fear of physical torture; or alluring, with sanctions appealing to our selfish nature by various forms of bribery; or spiritual, calling forth an untrammeled acceptance of itself by its inherent worth as self-authenticating. As James Denney has put it: "Where the human mind is concerned, it is idle to speak of an authority which can simply be imposed. . . . The real question is whether there is an authority that can impose itself, which can freely win the recognition and surrender of the mind and heart of man."[23] The character of God, it must be assumed, is such that He would never fall back on the mock authority of bribery. As Creator, He may at times have to exercise coercive authority over His rebellious creatures. As Watts' paraphrase of Psalm 100 puts it:

> Before Jehovah's awful throne,
> Ye nations, bow with sacred joy;
> Know that the Lord is God alone,
> He can create, and He destroy.

But God's authority is never full and final, never completely expressive of His nature as Seeking Holy Love, until it is a purely spiritual authority, the power of which lies in its glad acceptance by the believer. To quote Temple again: "The spiritual authority of God is that which He exercises by displaying not His power, but His character. Holiness, not omnipotence, is the spring of His spiritual authority. . . . The spiritual authority of God Himself consists, not in His having the power to create and to destroy, but in His being the appropriate object of worship and love."[24] Watts confirms this in the hymn just quoted. It is not only the fact that

> His sovereign power, without our aid,
> Made us of clay, and formed us men

that makes Him authoritative over us. His authority lies even more in this:

> And when like wandering sheep we strayed,
> He brought us to His fold again.

It is His seeking love that commands us. What then? This love is so inherently subduing, so radically self-authenticating, that the penitent, believing soul can make only one adequate response—glad acceptance and worship.

> We'll crowd His gates with thankful songs,
> High as the heavens our voices raise;

And earth, with her ten thousand tongues,
Shall fill His courts with sounding praise.

No better example of the response of the humble, believing heart to the authority of God could be found than that penned by Jonathan Edwards in his diary on Saturday, January 12, 1723. "I have this day," he said,

> solemnly renewed my baptismal covenant and self-dedication. . . . I have been before God; and have given myself, all that I am and have to God, so that I am not in any respect my own. I can claim no right in myself, no right in this understanding, this will, these affections that are in me; neither have I any right to this body or any of its members; no right to this tongue, these hands nor feet; no right to these senses, these eyes, these ears, this smell or taste. I have given myself clear away. . . . And I pray God, for the sake of Christ, to look upon it as a self-dedication; and to receive me now as entirely His own, and deal with me in all respects as such; whether He afflicts me or prospers me, or whatever He pleases to do with me, who am His. Now henceforth I am not to act in any respect as my own.[25]

When we speak of the authority of God over human life, we are speaking of this spiritual authority which by its very nature is final in that it authenticates itself and is wholly and gladly accepted by those over whom it is exercised.

This leads us to another question. If there is a gracious God who is Seeking Holy Love, and if because of His nature as God His will is sovereign over human life, where is that will to be found? Where does God, who exercises this authority over us, make Himself known? What is the channel of communication between God and us? There would seem to be four possible options in facing this question: (1) human reason; (2) religious experience; (3) the church; and (4) the Bible. Let us look at each of these in turn.

Human reason is a remarkable phenomenon. It has

achieved all the marvels of modern science and technology and for centuries has penetrated the mysteries of the thought world through philosophy. It is most certainly a part of "the image of God" in man which does not seem to be shared by the nonhuman animal world. Even Luther, who was deeply suspicious of the authority of reason in the sphere of religion, argued that "rightly understood, the reason of man is actually something divine. If it kept within its limits, and concentrated on what concerned it, it would be truly reasonable, and could not be too highly praised."[26] We would not champion irrationality, a religion wholly contrary to reason. If, for example, the Bible insisted that 2 + 2 equals 5, I should not take its authority for that, for that would be a flat contradiction of an axiom which any rational mind is forced to accept. We could not accept the word of Ignatius Loyola: "Laying aside all private judgment the spirit must always be ready to obey . . . the . . . church. Therefore, if anything shall appear white to our eyes which the church has defined as black, we likewise must declare it to be black."[27] The problem, however, is how adequate reason is in relating men to God. Can we believe that, as one writer put it, there is a "direct voice of God audible to us in the consecrated intelligence and conscience of men"[28] unaided from any other source?

For one thing, even in the area of science reason has its limitations. Scientific dogmas of the past have often been proved later to be merely ordered arrangements of our ignorance. I heard the president of the American Chemical Society say some time back that science today is very humble. It cannot be sure its facts are facts. All it can say is that this is the way things look to us from where we stand now, but we may be quite wrong. As P. T. Forsyth put it: "Is it not part of our intellectual duty to know the limits of our intellect?"[29] If reason is this limited, can it function adequately in the realm of the soul's relation to God? Can we risk our lives and our eternal destiny on mere rational contingencies? Would it not be well for us to accept Luther's caution that "the attempt to establish or defend divine order with human reason, unless that reason has previously been established and enlightened by faith, is just as futile as if I would try to throw light upon the sun with an unlighted lantern or rest a rock upon a reed"?[30]

Reason is inadequate in the realm of the soul not only because it is limited, but because it is perverse. The human mind is an instrument made to function in dependence on God. The mind of man is the mind of *fallen* man. Since man "refused to honour [God] as God, or to render him thanks," a "divine retribution" comes on "the godless wickedness of men." It is this: " . . . all their thinking has ended in futility, and their misguided minds are plunged in darkness" (Rom. 1:18-21, NEB). Luther echoed this when he said that

> Reason can not rightly accord [God] his deity nor attribute it to him as his own, though it rightly belongs to him alone. . . . Thus reason plays blindman's-buff with God and makes vain errors and always misses the mark, calling God what is not God, and not calling God what is God. . . . Thus it rushes in and accords the name and the divine honour, and the title, God, to what it thinks God is, and so never hits on the true God, but always finds the Devil or its own darkness, which the Devil rules.[31]

We cannot trust the authority of our own "darkened minds" in the region of the soul.

A third limitation of the reason is that it can deal only with ideas and concepts. It can merely argue from certain assumptions that God exists, and make rational guesses that if He exists, being God He should be such and such a kind of God. But these are all rational postulates limited to the realm of idea. But God is not a concept. He is a living Person. And the mystery of a living being cannot be penetrated merely by ideas about that being. One must know the person himself. It is impossible to enter the

secrets of another's life unless that other chooses to open
the inner door and make himself known in an act, or a
series of acts, of self-revelation. Hence, for the reason to
deal with impersonal abstractions, to approach God as
though He were an object for our observation, is futile.
God must make Himself known to us, as a Person to
persons, or we shall never know Him. He has done this in
Jesus Christ, where He confronts not only our reason but
the whole man. In this confrontation through the crucified
and risen Christ, we discover that the important thing is
not that we rationally know God, but that we are spiritually known by Him. It is a moral confrontation, where His
holiness suddenly reveals to us our sin. Then we cry out
with Isaiah, whose recoil from God was not that of a small
creature before an infinite Creator, but that of a great
sinner before absolute holiness: "Woe is me! For I am lost;
for I am a man of unclean lips and I dwell in the midst of a
people of unclean lips" (Isa. 6:5). The only adequate
response to a self-revealing God of holy seeking love is
penitence and faith, not merely thought.

A second option is the authority of experience. The
weakness of this position we will explore more fully in a
later chapter. Suffice it to say here that to rest on experience as a sure guide to the knowledge of God is a mere
psychological reliance of great danger. It is not my experience but *the thing experienced* that is important. And it is
well known that psychological moods may be induced by
various emotional states, or by synthetic emotional stimuli, or even by drugs, which experiences have no objective
reality corresponding to the subjective feelings. Rather
than putting us in contact with reality, they may be
escapes from reality. If God is a Person, I do not know
Him by *feeling* something about Him. We often have
feelings about other beings which turn out to be ill-
grounded and false. If I know God, He must make Himself
known to me as an objective Reality quite beyond my
experience of Him. When I know Him, I may of course

have feelings and experiences which come through fellow-ship with Him. But these are the result of His self-revela-tion, the outcome of fellowship with Him, and not the pathway of knowledge to Him. Our experiences are too tenuous, too changeable, too dependent on inner states and outer stimuli, to be finally trustworthy.

Testimony to this sometimes comes from surprising sources. In *God the Invisible King* H. G. Wells speaks of "that discontinuousness of our apparently homogeneous selves, the unincorporated and warring elements" within us. He continues:

> We are tripped up by forgetfulness, by distraction, by old habits, by tricks of appearance. There come dull patches of existence; those mysterious obliterations of one's finer sense that are due at times to the little minor poisons one eats or drinks, to phases of fatigue, ill-health, and bodily disorder, or one is betrayed by some unanticipated storm of emotion, brewed deep in the animal being and released by any trifling accident, such as personal jealousy or lust, or one is relaxed by contentment into vanity. All these rebel forces of our ill-co-ordinated selves, all these "disharmonies" of the inner being . . . carry us off to follies, offences, unkindness, waste, and leave us compromised, involved, and regretful, perplexed by a hundred difficulties we have put in our own way back to God.[32]

Do we really want to trust this bundle of disharmonious experiences as a channel of knowing God?

A third option is that the authority of God is mediated through the authority of the church. Since the church collected the authoritative books into the Bible, and be-cause of her nearly 2,000 years of experience, the weight of the church's authority is indeed great and must be highly respected. But can it be accepted as the final arbiter in matters of the soul? We shall also return to this question more fully in a later chapter. Let us simply say here that to make the church the final authority in matters of faith is impossible, even if we wanted so to do, because there is no

one church in all ages where unanimity in such matters is
to be found. There were wide varieties in the early church,
the Eastern Church broke from the Western in 1047, the
Protestant Churches broke from the Roman Church in
1517, and then the Protestant Churches splintered into
dozens of factions. Which is the church?

Furthermore, nearly all churches have reversed themselves at various times during their history. Which of their
judgments is then authoritative? If the latest and most
contemporary is chosen, then the authority of the church
would lie merely in the counting of contemporary noses,
with God in the control of a majority of fallible men at
any given Christian gathering.

Then, too, when we examine the history of the church
we find that in all its branches it has been all too human,
all too sinful, all too limited, all too fallible to be the
channel through which the final authority of God is mediated to men. God must make Himself known if He is to be
really known. And the church, with all its sin and schism,
must be under an authority outside herself by which her
own life is judged and her own destiny determined.

If neither reason, nor experience, nor the church can be
the trustworthy vehicle of God's self-revelation, what is
left? It would seem that the only other viable option is the
Bible. The Old and New Testaments are the written record
of the long conversation God had with His people over
1500 years or more, whereby in event and intimate fellowship He sought to open His heart to His people so that
they might know Him. From the call of Abraham some-
where near the year 2,000 B.C. to the birth, life, death,
and resurrection of Jesus in the first century of our era,
God was progressively breaking into the life of Israel and
the church with a redeeming love which, when it lays hold
of the human heart, is finally authoritative by commanding the allegiance which is the glad consequence of experienced redemption. Touch the great hearts of the Christian
church in every era, and you will find that the Bible was
accepted as authoritative because its message of God's

seeking, holy, redemptive love had subdued their natures and brought them to a glad acquiescence in the will of their Redeemer.

Listen to Paul in the first century: "For whatever was written in former days was written for our instruction, that by steadfastness and by the encouragement of the scriptures we might have hope" (Rom. 15:4). "Now to him who is able to strengthen you according to my gospel . . . according to the revelation of the mystery which was kept secret for long ages but is now disclosed and through the prophetic writings is made known . . . to the only wise God be glory for evermore through Jesus Christ! Amen" (Rom. 16:25-27).

Listen to Augustine at the end of the fourth century: "I was subdued by Thy books . . . when my wounds were touched by Thy healing fingers."[33]

Listen to Luther in the sixteenth century: "The Scriptures, although they . . . are written by men, are neither of men nor from men but from God."[34] "The Holy Scriptures are a vast and mighty forest, but there is not a single tree in it that I have not shaken with my own hand."[35] "Then I had the feeling that straight away I was born again, and had entered through open doors into paradise itself."[36]

And, finally, listen to Karl Barth in the twentieth century. When he visited America, it is reported that someone asked him what was the most majestic thought that had ever entered his mind. He replied:

> *Jesus loves me, this I know,*
> *For the Bible tells me so.*

The Bible has served through the centuries as the final authority over the soul, for the great and the small, the well known and the obscure, the learned and the unlearned, the rich and the poor, the living and the dying. It is doubtful that the changes wrought in our generation, great though they be, will effect any permanent change in this.

Chapter Two

The Bible

In the first chapter we saw that the problem of biblical
authority is a part of the larger problem of *any* authority
today. We saw that the question of biblical authority rests
on the question of the authority of God. We argued that if
there is a God, and man is a creature made to find the
meaning of his life in dependence on Him, then God is
authoritative over man. The nature of God, however,
makes His highest authority spiritual in character, and this
spiritual authority is so radically self-authenticating that
the penitent, believing man can respond only in glad acceptance and worship. For man to respond in this way, he
must discover who God is through the divine being's self-
revelation as Holy Seeking Love. Through what means has
God made Himself known? Among the options of human
reason, human experience, the church, and the Bible, we
chose the latter as the locus of this self-revelation. I would
like now to pursue further the question of the authority of
the Bible in its function as the vehicle of God's self-revelation.

Why is the Bible necessary to the soul's fellowship with
God? Because here and nowhere else do we have the
record of the historic process whereby God made Himself
known to man. The Bible is the record of the special
stream of holy history which ran through ancient history
as a whole as the Gulf Stream runs through the ocean.
Here God was at work making Himself known in a special

28

way through a special series of events. Of course, God was at work in all of history. He was Lord of Egypt and Babylon as well as of Israel. But His Lordship was not recognized outside Israel as it was within it. His providential works were over all people, but His *saving* deeds were done in Israel—at the Exodus and in all the ups and downs of Israel's history through nearly 2,000 years. Not that salvation was limited to Israel. It was for all nations. But all nations would have to know of it through what God had done for Israel. As God said through the great prophet of the exile: "Turn to me and be saved, all the ends of the earth! For I am God, and there is no other" (Isa. 45:22). But how were they to look unto Him? Through what He had done "for the sake of my servant Jacob, and Israel my chosen" (Isa. 45:4). When His preparatory work through Israel had been completed, "when the time had fully come, God sent forth his Son" (Gal. 4:4). This Son was sent to Israel, "for salvation is from the Jews" (John 4:22). But these same Jews were to be "witnesses" of "all that Jesus began to do and teach" in the days of His flesh to "the end of the earth" (Acts 1:1, 8). God's holy seeking love is therefore known through the special series of events which took place in the narrow stream of Israel's history from Abraham to Jesus Christ. Since these events are recorded in the Bible, and nowhere else, the Bible becomes forever the source and norm of the Christian faith. The heart of the faith is this story through which we know God and through which we make our response to Him. If we lost the Bible, we would lose the story. And if we lost the story, the Christian faith would be at an end.

This is expressed with great force by H. H. Farmer, who insisted that since Christianity is at heart an absolutely "unique, decisive . . . final, completely adequate, wholly indispensable" event, it could never have been discovered by human reflection, for reflection cannot produce an event. "An event can only establish itself — by happening!

... And it can only become generally known ... by the story being told."[1] Dr. Farmer illustrates his point by proposing that we imagine the Hindu religion obliterated from the mind of man — not one Hindu left, not one copy of Hindu sacred writings, not one record in extant history that there ever was such a thing as Hinduism. Given this situation, it is conceivable that Hinduism could arise again, within five years, or fifty years, or five hundred years. For Hinduism is basically a way of thinking, a way of looking at life. If men thought this way once, it is conceivable that other men could think this same way at a later time. But imagine Christianity obliterated — not one living Christian, not one copy of the Christian Scriptures, not one mention in extant history that Christianity had ever existed. Given this situation, it is inconceivable that Christianity could ever arise again. For Christianity basically is a story, the story of God's special dealings in history from Abraham to Jesus Christ. It is to this story that Christians respond in faith, love and obedience, and this story is found only in the Bible. The Bible is indispensable. Christianity is a historic religion. It is a "given." It comes to us. We are free to accept it, but not to remake or modify it. Since it comes to us through the Bible, the Bible is therefore authoritative as the only record of the saving events by which the Christian faith was brought into being. Karl Barth wrote:

> Even the smallest, strangest, simplest or obscurest among the biblical witnesses has an incomparable advantage over even the most pious, scholarly, and sagacious latter-day theologian. From his special point of view and in his special fashion, the witness has thought, spoken and written about the revelatory Word and act in direct confrontation with it. All subsequent theology, as well as the whole of the community that comes after the event, will never find itself in the same immediate confrontation.[2]

But did not the church produce the Bible? If so, would not the church which produced the Bible be authoritative over it? At least two things must be said about this. First, it is true that the church existed before the Bible and that the books of the Bible were collected and preserved by the church. In reality, however, the church did not bring the Bible into being, nor did the Bible bring the church into being. It was the *message* of the Bible, the *gospel,* which produced both the church and the Bible. The content of the Bible was a *gospel* before it was a book. This is clearly borne out in the Westminster Confession of Faith, where we read: " . . . It pleased the Lord, at sundry times, and in divers manners, to reveal himself, and to declare . . . his will unto his church; and *afterwards* . . . to commit the same wholly unto writing" (italics mine; I:1). It is the declaration of God's will in historic events "at sundry times, and in divers manners" that constitutes the gospel. *Afterwards* it was made a matter of record. The gospel antedates the record of it. The record is authoritative, therefore, not because the church produced it but because it is the record of that gospel which produced the church, and which continues to nourish her life. As Luther put it: "The church is the daughter born of the Word, not the mother of the Word."[3]

The second thing to be said is this: For the church to select certain books as authoritative and to bind them together into a Bible was not to give those books authority. It is one thing to *bestow* authority, it is another to *recognize* it. For the church to recognize the authority of the gospel in the books which she chose as her Bible does not place the church above these books. In fact, in developing a canon of Scripture at all, the early church demonstrated that she was fully aware that she herself was not authoritative. Had she assumed herself to be authoritative, she would not have raised over herself a particular group of books as the norm by which she and the church of the future would be judged.

In declaring the books of the Bible authoritative over her life, the church was but witnessing to the historic nature of her faith and the uniqueness of the saving events by which she was brought into being and by which she was to be forever nurtured. If revelation were merely ideas, it is conceivable that men might get better or more refined ideas through the discipline and experience of the years. The works of Augustine, or Aquinas, or Luther, or Calvin might be added to the biblical record. But, as H. Scott Holland has said, " . . . The whole body of spiritual experience dates from an original experience which cannot but possess the authority which belongs to it through being, by its very nature, unique. . . . Blessed indeed are they that have not seen, and yet have believed. . . . But they can only arrive at this blessing through the witness of those who believed because they saw. They have no other means of acquiring it."[4] It was the apostolic generation, and they alone, who could say to us: "It was there from the beginning; we have heard it; we have seen it with our own eyes; we looked upon it, and felt it with our own hands; and it is of this we tell. . . . What we have seen and heard we declare to you, so that you and we together may share in a common life" (I John 1:1, 3, NEB). We can receive our faith only from those who "touched and handled."

The strongest witness to this is the attitude toward the Bible held by those great Christian spirits whose writings would be added to it were it not unique. Augustine is certainly one of these, and he once wrote to St. Jerome: "Dear brother, I hope that you do not expect your books to be regarded as equal to those of the apostles and prophets. God forbid that you should desire such a thing."[5] Of his own works he said: " . . . Do not follow my writing as you do Holy Scripture. Instead, whatever you find in Holy Scripture that you would not have believed before, believe without doubt. But in my writings you should regard nothing as certain that you were uncertain about before, unless I have proved its truth."[6] St. Bernard once compared the Scriptures to a spring and the writings of later Fathers to a brook which flowed from it.

He insisted that only a fool would drink from the brook when he could drink from the spring, and that the function of the brook is to lead one to the spring. The value of later Christian writers, then, if they have any worth, is to lead back to the Bible. Luther once said that he "would be ashamed to death"[7] if anybody ever regarded his books as equal to those of the apostles and prophets. In fact, he resisted for long any attempt to publish a collection of his works:

> I wish all my books were extinct, so that only the sacred books in the Bible would be diligently read.... For all other writing is to lead the way into and point toward the Scriptures, ... in order that each person may drink of the fresh spring himself, as all those fathers who wanted to accomplish something good had to do.... Therefore it behooves us to let the prophets and apostles stand at the professor's lectern, while we, down below at their feet, listen to what they say. It is not they who must hear what we say.[8]

James Denney put the matter well when he said: "There has been no interpretation of the revelation made in Jesus which has done more than try to grasp the breadth and depth of apostolic teaching; and the perennial impulse which Scripture and Scripture alone communicates to spiritual life and spiritual thought is always sealing its pre-eminence anew."[9] The Bible stands, and always shall, as the unique record of the unique and unrepeatable deeds by which the church came into being, and from which her life, till the end of the world, will be nurtured and judged.

But how must we approach this book so that its inherent, self-authenticating, spiritual authority may grip us and command us? How do we get beyond mere theory to the point where the Bible's authority begins to function in our lives? A complete answer to this is beyond our comprehension. There is a mystery about the authority of the Bible over the human spirit, as profound as the mystery of God. As we have said, if the Bible has any inherent authority it is because it is the vehicle of God's authority. And who can define the mystery of the approach of God to the human soul? His is an authority which defies "our ability to localize or define and which by the same token is beyond our control, but whose presence is as sure as the rising of the sun."[10]

Insofar as we can think our way into this problem at all, we can establish, it seems to me, two major aspects. One has to do with the Bible, the other has to do with ourselves. One is objective, the other subjective. The problem is how to approach the Bible so that we may hear God's voice speaking to us through it. The Bible is the medium through which God speaks. We are the listeners. In order to allow the Bible to perform its proper function, we must know something about the medium and we must also know how to listen. Let us look first at the Bible as the medium of God's voice.

It is well to point out initially that our concern with the Bible should be more with its function than with itself. That is, the God to whom it bears witness should be central in our interest rather than the instrument through which that witness comes. The worth of the Scriptures is determined by their power to convey the voice of God. It is not the Bible which speaks, but God who speaks through the Bible. Our whole attention in studying the Bible, therefore, should be given to listening for the voice of God through it.

The function of a light bulb, for example, is to be the medium of producing light. The bulb is not the light, yet you do not have the light without the bulb. Its value to us, however, does not lie in looking at the bulb itself, nor even in understanding its nature. Its value is that light comes through it, enabling us to see in the darkness. Likewise, the value of a lens in a telescope is that it enables us to see the stars.

The Bible is the instrument through which God speaks, the means by which His light is cast upon life, the lens through which we see "him who is invisible." If we turn our attention to the Bible itself rather than to the voice, the light, and the God from whom they come, we should be putting the Bible in the place of God, and thus turning it into an idol. Even if the instrument should in places seem to us to be faulty, and to distort the voice of God in some measure, still its excellence lies in its power to convey to us, even in distorted fashion, the authentic voice of God. There are those who prefer to hear the voice of Alma Gluck through the imperfect recordings made in her time, than to hear the voices of most modern singers through the vastly superior recordings of today. These people are convinced that her voice, even when distorted, had a superb quality that is unmatched by most other voices heard clearly. And if her voice is to be heard today, it must be heard through these imperfect recordings. So it is with the voice of God. It is better to hear His voice, though faintly and amid scratches and other extraneous sounds, than to hear any other voice. And if we are to hear it, we must listen for it through the Bible, which is the only available record of His speaking "to our fathers by the prophets" and His final word "to us by a Son" (Heb. 1:1, 2).

The second thing to say about the Bible is that we should listen through it only for that which it is designed to speak. The Bible exists to tell us — what we can find out in no other way — about God, about ourselves, and about the interrelations between God and us. In other words, the Bible is a *religious* book, and should be asked to yield answers to nothing but religious questions. It is interesting how unselfconscious the Bible writers seem to be about their own writing. The Bible seldom speaks of itself or of its role in human life. But when it does, it seems to speak solely about its dynamic function in making God known, in revealing man to himself, and in repairing the broken relationships between the two.

The classic passage in this regard is II Timothy 3:15, 16.

There the writer speaks of a twofold function of the Scriptures. First, they "are able to instruct you for salvation through faith in Christ Jesus." Second, they are "profitable for teaching, for reproof, for correction, and for training in righteousness, that the man of God may be complete, equipped for every good work." Here we see that the Scriptures are "able," or as the New English Bible puts it, they "have power," to lead men into a saving knowledge of God in Christ, and that they then continue to function by leading the Christian to a mature understanding of the truth and by leading him in a life of good works.

These functions are stated in other places as well. In Romans 16:25, 26 Paul says that "the prophetic writings," that is, the Old Testament, were the bearers of the "mystery" of salvation designed "to bring about obedience to the faith." In the same letter he says that the Scriptures function by producing "hope" in the believer (15:4). Twice in Acts Paul is described as using the Scriptures to show that "Jesus . . . is the Christ" (17:3; 18:28). In the Fourth Gospel, Jesus says that the Scriptures "bear witness to [Him]" (5:39). Luke tells us that the risen Lord, "beginning with Moses and all the prophets . . . interpreted to them in all the scriptures the things concerning himself" (Luke 24:27). There seems to be a unanimous witness, in the few places where the Scriptures speak of their own function, that they exist to proclaim the gospel and lead men to Christ, and that they are to be judged solely by their power to do this.

Luther grasped this clearly when he said that the New Testament was "but a public preaching and proclamation of Christ, set forth through the sayings of the Old Testament and fulfilled through Christ. . . . Here you will find the swaddling cloths and the manger in which Christ lies, and to which the angel points the shepherds. Simple and lowly are these swaddling cloths, but dear is the treasure, Christ, who lies in them."[11]

The Westminster Confession supports Luther at this point when it describes the function of Scripture as giving "that knowledge of God, and of his will, which is necessary unto salvation" (I, 1). It further describes the Scriptures as giving "the whole counsel of God, concerning all things necessary for his own glory, man's salvation, faith, and life" (I, 6).

The Scriptures themselves, then, and these guides to its understanding, suggest that we are making proper use of the Bible only when we are asking it questions about God, His will, His glory, and man's salvation, faith, and life.

How often the Bible is misused by being used for other ends. I was once told by a man that the dimensions of Noah's ark are the perfect dimensions for boat building, implying that the art of boat building was a matter of divine revelation. I know nothing about the proper dimensions of boats, but if my friend's judgment is true, I should attribute it to the fact that either Noah, or whoever wrote down the story, was a skilled builder of boats rather than that the dimensions were given by divine inspiration. What a needless struggle was set up in the days of Galileo by turning the Bible into a book of astronomy; and in the days of Darwin, by turning it into a book of biological science. In matters of science, ask the scientist. In matters of religion, ask the Bible. It is a sure guide about that — and nothing else. It may have accompanying historical and geographical information, but these are of value in showing where and when God did His saving work for man. They are incidental to their religious significance. The Bible is time-conditioned and limited in other spheres, often reflecting the naive scientific world-view of its time and filled with much that is the accompaniment of the Word of God rather than a witness to God. There is much in the Bible, particularly in the early strands of the Old Testament, that must be judged by the gospel and Christ. It must not be confused with the gospel and the will of Christ. There is much that is frame rather than painting.

There is much that is scaffolding rather than building. There is much that is dark background rather than shining light. Luther put this boldly when he said, "The pure Scripture must be separated from their dregs and filth; which it has ever been my aim to do, that the divine truths may be looked upon in one light, and the trifles of these men in another."[12] Let us not, therefore, stumble over such idle and futile questions as where Cain got his wife, whether the six days of creation in Genesis were twenty-four-hour days, and whether Noah's flood covered the whole earth or just the Mesopotamian area, the answer to which is quite irrelevant to God's will to save us in Christ, and our need to respond to His saving action in faith and obedience.

A third thing that must be kept in mind about the Bible is that it is language *and* literature. As language, it must be read in the light of what its original words meant, not what we think they meant or what we should like them to have meant. And as literature it must be interpreted at each particular place in accord with the type of literature with which we are dealing. We cannot interpret poetry as prose, drama as history, parable as detailed theological writing, apocalyptic as literal. This means that language and literature must be taken seriously. Luther said: "Although the gospel came and still comes to us through the Holy Spirit alone, we cannot deny that it came through the medium of languages, was spread abroad by that means, and must be preserved by the same means."[13] He added that it was a great "sin and loss that we do not study languages. . . ."[14] He added later: "I would surely have never flushed a covey if the languages had not helped me and given me a sure and certain knowledge of Scripture."[15] Luther also took into account the various literary forms of the Bible, recognizing that details of dramatic form were to be understood as such and not made the basis of theological interpretation, and refusing to interpret the Bible allegorically unless he was dealing with allegory. Any of us can go far toward examining the type of literature embodied in any particular passage; where we do not have access to the original languages, we can examine several translations in English and compare them, and seek help in other works about the exact meaning of words.

One further thing about the Bible itself, and that is that we should deal with it in its broad sweep, not merely in snippets. It is well known that isolated sentences, taken out of context, can be twisted to almost any purpose. It is well known, too, that the Bible itself has differences of emphasis in various places which, if taken alone, would be either partial truth or perverted truth. These need the wholeness and balance of the "harmonious opposites" to be found in other passages of Scripture. Here again the Westminster Confession offers wise counsel: "The infallible rule of interpretation of Scripture, is the Scripture itself; and therefore, when there is a question about the true and full sense of any scripture (which is not manifold, but one), it may be searched and known by other places that speak more clearly" (I, 9). The truth, then, is not merely the partial truth of any one word of Scripture, but the truth to be drawn from the whole sweep of the biblical drama, culminating in Jesus Christ.

Now we come to the more subjective side of the question — to the reader, the listener for the voice of God through Scripture. Even though a voice should echo loudly through the forest, there is no hearing if all within earshot are deaf. Communication involves hearing as well as speaking. Jesus sensed this when several times He said to His listeners, "Take heed then how you hear" (Luke 8:18). God speaks. How do we men hear?

The first suggestion I would make is that if God speaks through the Bible, we should listen for His voice *there*. We can only hear where He has chosen to speak. I may have preferred Him to speak elsewhere, but if the Bible is where He has spoken, that is where I must listen. We should not, therefore, despair of hearing the voice of God through the

Scriptures until we have exposed ourselves to them directly and faithfully in order that they may do their work in our lives. But how few do any regular or systematic reading or study of the Bible!

Some years ago, the late D. T. Niles of Ceylon was on shipboard. When, in conversation with him, a group of young people discovered that he was a minister, they immediately began to attack the Christian faith. He said that he had not been in the confrontation long before it became apparent that the most vocal one in the group was totally ignorant of the Christianity he was supposedly rejecting. After a while, Dr. Niles forced him to admit that he had never so much as read even one of the Gospels. Dr. Niles then told the group that they could carry the discussion no further until they sufficiently informed themselves about what they were denouncing to carry on an intelligent interchange of thought. This situation is perhaps more typical than we suppose. The Bible is a best seller. It is not a best read book.

And even those of us who would like to understand its meaning are more inclined to read books about the Bible than to read the Bible itself. Now consulting secondary sources may be worthy, for the Bible is a difficult book. We need to help each other understand it, and there are those whose training or whose deep and long experience with the Scriptures gives them eyes to see what we may miss. The study of responsible word books, commentaries, and devotional literature, then, may be extremely helpful in enabling us to hear the voice of God through the Bible. While Luther and Calvin put the Bible into the language of the people, they also wrote commentaries to try to help the people understand it. We have already seen, however, that Luther's aim in writing books was to throw such light on the Bible that people would finally leave his books and go back to the Bible itself.

There is no way to mediate the throb of any great book save through the book itself. Emile Cammaerts tells of spending a summer reading through Dante's *Divine Comedy* with his Mother. He writes: "I remember the armchair in which she sat in a shady corner of our small garden, her keen pale face framed in a halo of thin red hair, and the impatience she showed when I struggled too long over the notes of various commentators who did not always agree: 'Oh! Leave your notes alone,' she exclaimed, 'can't you *hear*?' "[16] She wanted him to listen not to what others said about Dante, but to Dante himself. A minister friend has told me how he used to hate Calvin, whom he knew only through his interpreters. One day he decided that it was unfair for him to judge Calvin at second-hand; he would read him directly. After a careful study of the great theologian himself, he came out with a profound admiration for his work and a permanent mark on his own life and ministry.

How much better off would we be if we had the patience and the determination to come to the Bible directly, to listen for the voice of God there. As we have already said, and shall see later, there is nothing wrong with using helps to Bible study. They are necessary. But either before using these helps, or after, or both, we owe it to ourselves and to the Bible to sit before it with all our powers of heart and mind alert, listening for the voice of God to our spirits. It might be surprising what would happen through this process. Then we might join the friends of the Samaritan woman who said: "It is no longer because of what you said that we believe, for we have heard him ourselves; and we know that this is in truth the Saviour of the world" (John 4:42).

During the Hitler regime in Germany, Dietrich Bonhoeffer, who was later martyred, conducted an illegal Preachers' Seminary for some months. One who participated in it tells that after the "external shock" of the barren surroundings and bleak existence was overcome, they experienced an "inner shock":

> In the mornings, there was half an hour of silent meditation on
> one biblical text in Luther's translation; the same text for a
> week. We were not allowed to consult the original text, a
> dictionary or other books during this period. . . . What we
> experienced, however, at least at the beginning, was emptiness
> in ourselves and in the texts, where knowledge and answers
> had been promised to us. . . . The time of meditation . . . did
> not grow into a time of revelation; the text did not speak to
> us, and if it did, it was in our own voice.

Bonhoeffer kept them at it, however, although he finally
permitted them "to meditate together, and not in silence,
once or twice a week."[17] After long periods of this discipline, the word began to break through. The writer says:

> We had not known what it means that the word preaches
> itself. . . . Only through long times of waiting and quiet did we
> learn that the text "may be our master." Half an hour of
> concentration: it is amazing what comes into your head during
> that time. . . . For many of us that half hour remained a
> burden to the end. But it taught all of us that the biblical word
> is more than a "subject" which can be handled *ad libitum* [just
> as one wishes] .[18]

Maybe God would speak to us in the Scriptures if we
should put ourselves within hearing distance.

Another, and exceedingly important, requisite to hearing God's voice in Scripture is a humble spirit that is
willing to acknowledge its own inadequacy of mind and
heart, that is willing to be taught, that is willing to confess
through prayer that it is only with the help of the Holy
Spirit that the Bible may become the vehicle of the voice
of God. As the Westminster Confession says, " . . . Our full
persuasion and assurance of the infallible truth and divine
authority [of Holy Scripture] is from the inward work of
the Holy Spirit, bearing witness by and with the word in
our hearts" (I, 5). Are we willing to grant this, to allow
that natively we cannot hear the voice of God; that He
must open our ears to His word; that only by the action of

His Spirit, shattering all our self-sufficiency and pride, can we have converse with Him?

The critical study of the Bible raises a thousand problems for the modern mind. These are often used as excuses for not trusting the Scriptures, as though our difficulties with them were mainly intellectual. One wonders whether our problems are not more deeply rooted in our pride and hardness of heart. Jesus once said to His disciples when they failed to understand Him, "Do you not yet perceive or understand? Are your hearts hardened?" (Mark 8:17). And the writer to the Hebrews pleaded: "Today, when you hear his voice, do not harden your hearts" (3:15). Do not our difficulties with the Bible spring more from a self-centered, humanistic world view which has little or no place for God than from our intellectual difficulties? In the words of P. T. Forsyth, "It is the wills of men, and not their views, that are the great obstacle to the Gospel."[19] Or as George W. Richards put it: "The offense of the gospel is not against the intellect but against the heart of man."[20] E. C. Blackman has said: " . . . The common assumption is that there is no source of authority outside the stream of history itself and the sum total of human experience. The issue is between humanism in all its varieties . . . and the transcendentalism of Christian faith, with its assurance that there is light from on high for man's darkness, and its warning that man's authority is not in himself, but in God."[21]

> *The angels keep their ancient places;—*
> *Turn but a stone, and start a wing!*
> *'Tis ye, 'tis your estranged faces,*
> *That miss the many-splendoured thing.*[22]

What is needed most is not the criticism that is demanded of the mind — though that has its worth — but the criticism which moves in the realm of redemption. Are we willing to allow God to redeem us in His Son? If so, then the Bible would speak to our redeemed souls with authority. Again as P. T. Forsyth put it: "The most present and real fact of our Christian faith is the fact accessible to faith alone. It is the fact that Christ has brought us God and destroyed our guilt. You do not yet know the inner Christ who are but His lovers or friends. You need to have been His patients and to owe Him your life. That is Christianity."[23]

One of the strange passages in the New Testament casts its light at this point. In the final conflict between Jesus and His enemies at the close of His life, He was asked: "By what authority are you doing these things, or who gave you this authority to do them?" (Mark 11:28). Jesus made a strange reply: "I will ask you a question; answer me, and I will tell you by what authority I do these things. Was the baptism of John from heaven or from men? Answer me." When, after some deliberation with each other, they replied, "We do not know," Jesus then said: "Neither will I tell you by what authority I do these things" (Mark 11:29-33). Unless we think that our Lord was playing a clever word game with them, engaging in merely a "skillful maneuver" to best them in an argument, this strange passage suggests that there is some vital connection between the authority of Jesus and the authority of John. This is to be seen at one level in the fact that the voice of prophecy had been silenced in Israel for three or four centuries. Its reappearance in John the Baptist was in itself, according to their own tradition, one of the signs of the approach of the Messianic Age. Furthermore, John had borne direct witness to Jesus as the Coming One. If John's testimony were authentic, belief in his message would have pointed to Jesus as the Messiah.

There is a deeper element here, however. What was the baptism of John? It was "a baptism of repentance for the forgiveness of sins" (Mark 1:4). It insisted that man is in the wrong with God; that in himself man has no power to bring about his own fulfillment; that the whole prophetic movement climaxed in John had held out hopes that man-

kind could not achieve and had set ideals which there was
no human dynamic adequate to fulfil. As H. Scott Holland
has put it so profoundly, the "crucial discovery" made by
John the Baptist

> was the nature of the limit set on the upward movement of
> humanity. That movement went so far; achieved so much; was
> full of such heroic possibilities; suggested, promised, fostered
> such high hopes. Yet, out of itself, it could not attain to its
> own proper crown and culmination. It worked up towards a
> fulfilment which was beyond its own powers. . . . Man is not,
> himself, in possession of that which should complete his man-
> hood. He waits for something more — for an entry, for an
> arrival. There is that which comes from beyond, from afar. It
> enters in upon him, it takes possession, it lifts, it quickens, it
> transfigures, it fulfils. . . . He is most himself when he is most
> surrendered to this other.[24]

The problem, then, is this: "Has man power to deliver
himself? Can he wrestle himself away out of his sin, by
development from within? If he can, then the Baptist
made a mistake; he falsified experience."[25] If, however, he
was right, then John's prophetic authority confronts us
with a decision. Are we willing to admit our own sin,
failure, and need? Does our inner nature yearn for a
fulfillment which we ourselves have no power to achieve? Is
this yearning to remain forever unanswered? Or, is there
One who comes to us with a redemptive love which is
more than a match for our yearning, with a consummation
of meaning that forever brands Him as authoritative, as the
One whose authority rests in the fact that He "has brought
God's life to me"? In other words, am I willing first to
accept the authority of John — the demand for "repentance for the forgiveness of sins" — which, if accepted,
leads directly to Jesus Christ as the Forgiver of those sins,
whose authority then needs no explanation or defense —
only glad acceptance and surrender?

We come back, then, to where we began. The problem
of biblical authority is the problem of the authority of

God over man. And since God has chosen to make Himself known to us in His Son, the problem of biblical authority must ultimately be answered by facing the question put by Jesus to His disciples: "But who do you say that I am?" (Mark 8:29). This is brought to a focus in another passage from P. T. Forsyth. After granting that we need historical criticism, that literary criticism has its rights, that psychological criticism is worthy, he says:

> But allowing for all such things, the question remains dogmatic, was He, is He, what Christian faith essentially believed? Did these convictions, of His and of the Church, correspond to reality? Was He, is He, in God what He thought He was and what He was held to be? When the first Church worshiped Him with God's name, and set Him on God's throne, were they a new race of idolaters? Was His influence so poor in quality that it could not protect from that? He thought Himself redeemer; did He really redeem? Did God redeem in Him? Was God the real actor in His saving action? These are the questions; and in all such questions, criticism is *ultra vires* [beyond its power]. These things are settled in another and higher court.... The soundest criticism is the criticism by a believing Church, daily living on the Grace of the Cross and the venture of faith.... The real criticism ... is not our criticism of Christ, but Christ's criticism of us, His saving judgment of us.[26]

It was facing such questions as these which led Forsyth to say: "I was turned from a Christian to a believer, from a lover of love to an object of grace."[27]

Are we, or are we willing to be, believers and objects of grace? If so, we shall find Christ in the Scriptures, and He will be the touchstone of their authority for us. Then we shall understand what Sir Walter Scott meant when, as he lay dying, he said to his son-in-law, Lockhart: "Bring me the book." "What book?" asked Lockhart. "*The* book," said Sir Walter; "the Bible; there is but one."[28]

Chapter Three

The Authority of the Old Testament

The problem of the authority of the Old Testament for the Christian church is an old and difficult one. It deserves serious wrestling, however, and not the cavalier treatment it often gets. H. G. Wells, for example, in *God the Invisible King,* gives the Old Testament short shrift with a superficial wave of the hand unworthy of one as learned and gifted as he. Dr. H. Scott Holland wrote of Wells' estimate of the Old Testament:

> It hardly reaches the level of a platform orator in Victoria Park. It flings mud about, like a street arab. It does not offer itself to sane discussion. A ribald taunt about a Syrian God of Vengeance, or the obscenity of circumcision, is enough to dispose of the Old Testament, and the religion of Israel. The memory of a nurserymaid who filled his childhood with terror of a "bogey" God, bent on catching him out, and punishing him, dismisses the idea of the Christian God.[1]

Holland comments:

> I always wonder at the strange persistence of these nurserymaids, who spread this secret teaching, like some dark Ophite sect, burrowing below the standard Faith. These are always turning up in biographies, though I never have met them in real life. If anybody like Mr. Wells is born, they hurry off to his cradle and darken and dog his child years — while, all the time, for generation after generation, thousands upon thou-

sands of happy children are trooping along without a shadow of fear upon their white souls, while they sing: —

> *There's a Friend for little children*
> *Above the bright blue sky,*
> *A Friend Who never changes*
> *Whose love will never die.*

. . . Can anything be more soothing, and tender, and free from alarm? That is the normal standardized Christianity of our nurseries. We really must stifle the last nurserymaid of this dark Manichaean guild, if there is still one on the prowl.[2]

One fears that this shallow, uninformed, and benighted outlook on the Old Testament is typical of the way many regard this greatest collection of books save the New Testament, and a collection of books without which the New Testament cannot be properly understood.

This easy discarding of the Old Testament is an old problem. One of the earliest heretics to appear in the church was Marcion, who lived and wrote in the early decades of the second century. He removed the Old Testament completely from the Christian Bible and expurgated much from the New Testament that he thought had an Old Testament flavor. For him, the God of the Old Testament and the God of the New were totally different beings, and the Old Testament God had to go. The church, of course, rejected his view and in response began to collect the sacred books that would be authoritative over her life. In this process the church never for one moment wavered in the determination to keep the Old Testament as a part of the Christian Bible.

The problem did not die there, however. It has cropped up at various times throughout Christian history. Luther, for example, found it in his day:

There are some who have little regard for the Old Testament. They think of it as a book that was given to the Jewish people only and is now out of date, containing only stories of past times. They think they have enough in the New Testament. . . . I beg and really caution every pious Christian not to be offended by the simplicity of the language and stories frequently encountered there, but fully realize that . . . these are the very words, works, judgments, and deeds of the majesty, power, and wisdom of the most high God. For these are the Scriptures which make fools of all the wise and understanding, and are open only to the small and simple.[3]

In recent times, the problem of the Old Testament came to a focus again in the Christian liberalism of the end of the nineteenth and the beginning of the twentieth century. To the liberals, the Old Testament was an embarrassment. They preferred not to have to carry the weight of trying to justify it to the modern world. They felt, therefore, that it should be kept in libraries for the study of historians of religion, but that it should not be used in the life and worship of the Christian church. This is the practical, if not the reasoned, view of many Christians today, who seldom read the Old Testament and think of it merely as preparatory to the New Testament, which, as the shell of the egg is abandoned when the chick is hatched, may now be forgotten.

The Old Testament has made too significant an impact on the life of the world to be given such cavalier treatment. As H. Scott Holland added about Wells' supercilious attitude:

Mr. Wells must learn that the fate of Israel is to be judged, not by the wild racial conceptions of Syrian deities from out of which it began, but by the heights to which, in spite of such a beginning, it actually rose. When he has shown that he can take account of the Twenty-third, or the Ninetieth, or Ninety-first, or One-hundred-and-fourth Psalms, or of the Second Isaiah, with its vision of the sacrificial Servant, the ideal Israel, who is ready for exile, suffering, ruin, death, if only, by his sacrifice, he may carry light to the Gentiles who are his slayers, it will be time to consider what he has to say about the Old Testament.[4]

Apart from the New Testament, which as we have noted and shall discuss later does not stand without the Old Testament, has there been any literature produced in the history of the human race that has scaled the heights of the human spirit or plumbed the depths of the human heart as the Old Testament has done? And apart from Jesus of Nazareth, whose God was the God of the Old Testament, where can one find any picture of God equal to that of the Hebrew prophets? And who has left his mark on the rising and falling generations as have they? John Oman spoke well when he said:

> . . . In comparison with them, the influence of kings and conquerors has been superficial and fleeting. They were weak, but out of weakness were made strong. They were often destroyed, but their destruction was their victory. Though humble and poor, lacking all the advantages of possession and of place, uncrowned by any dignity except the glory of their own faithfulness, they were yet set over the nations and over the kingdoms, to pluck up and to break down, to destroy and to overthrow, to build and to plant. Vast armies marched up and down with noise and tumult. Men were used in masses as mere pawns to play with in the game of might and dread. The prophets stood alone. . . . While the thunder of the armies has passed like the roar of the billows that waste their strength on a rock-bound coast, their word still echoes through the fruitful earth like the murmur of still fertilizing streams. . . . No terror could subjugate their souls. . . . Vast calamities came upon their nation and upon themselves. . . . loss of goods and loss of friends, destruction of country, dissolution of society, scorn and slavery and death. . . . Upon the prophets all these calamities came, and the result was not dismay, but right thoughts of God's ways, right trust in God's help, right views of God's purpose . . . . Trial could not daunt them, nor opposition dismay; submission for them was strength and obedience peace. Being free in God, nothing could make them slaves in God's world.[5]

If we lost all pre-Christian literature but the Old Testament, would the light on life be any the less bright? Would we know any the less how to live and how to die? Is there, then, not an authentic voice of God in these Scriptures for the Christian church, which we should lose at our peril? Let us look at the evidence for this judgment.

First, the Old Testament was the Bible of Jesus. He had no other. If there were ever One who could afford to dismiss the Old Testament, it would have been He, given the claims made for Him earlier in this book. He did not do so, however, but used them continually, and held them in the highest esteem. Therefore, as James Denney has said, "in a very real sense His authority may be invoked" to authenticate the Old Testament as having Christian value.[6]

Jesus Himself was a product of the community of faith nurtured by the Old Testament. The songs at the Annunciation of the birth of Jesus set Him in a direct relationship with that community. Mary sings that in the promised birth of Jesus, God "has helped his servant Israel, in remembrance of his mercy, as he spoke to our fathers, to Abraham and to his posterity forever" (Luke 1:54, 55). Simeon connects His birth with the history of Israel when he says, "Behold, this child is set for the fall and rising of many in Israel" (Luke 2:34), and refers to Him as "a light for revelation to the Gentiles, and for glory to thy people Israel" (Luke 2:32). These songs also relate His birth to the long deferred hope kindled by the Old Testament for "the consolation of Israel" (Luke 2:25), "the redemption of Jerusalem" (Luke 2:38). There is in all of these passages a strong awareness that the birth of Jesus was no isolated event, but a happening whose significance is to be seen only in relation to the earlier events depicted in the Old Testament.

Furthermore, it is plain that Jesus nourished His own faith in the Scriptures, finding them a source of fellowship with God. In every crisis or otherwise important moment in His life, the Old Testament emerges in a fashion to suggest that it was by its light that He lived, and that it was through its pages that He heard the voice of His God. For example, in the struggle of His soul at His baptism, the resolution of the issue comes through God speaking to His inner life by means of two Old Testament passages—Psalm 2 and Isaiah 42. In the dark moments of conflict recorded in the temptation story, in each case Jesus won the victory over the Tempter by a word from the Old Testament (Luke 4:1-13). When in a moment of deep distress John the Baptist challenged the authenticity of Jesus' mission, the Lord answered by referring him to two passages in the prophecy of Isaiah and then proceeded to interpret John's mission to those around Him in terms of Malachi's promise of Elijah's coming (Luke 7:18-28). At the Great Confession, Jesus sought to interpret the meaning of the Messiahship they had just confessed by referring to the Suffering Servant depicted in Isaiah 42 to 53 (Luke 9:18-22). At the Last Supper, He spoke of His death in relation to the Old Testament covenant of God's grace (Mark 14:24). In his supreme agony on the cross, Jesus found expression for the bitterness of His soul in the twenty-second Psalm (Mark 15:34).

Jesus also affirms the authority of the Old Testament more directly. In the Sermon on the Mount, He says: ". . . Till heaven and earth pass away, not an iota, not a dot, will pass from the law until all is accomplished" (Matt. 5:18). In His sermon at His home-town synagogue, He said: "Today this scripture has been fulfilled in your hearing" (Luke 4:21). In discussions with His opponents, on various occasions, He said: "Have you never read in the scriptures?" (Matt. 21:42). "You are wrong, because you know neither the scriptures nor the power of God" (Matt. 22:29). "You search the scriptures . . . and it is they that bear witness to me" (John 5:39). In discussing the question of whether men might be startled into belief in God by the appearance of one from the dead, He said: "They have Moses and the prophets. . . . If they do not hear Moses and the prophets, neither will they be convinced if some one should rise from the dead" (Luke 16:29, 31). When Peter sought to defend Him in the garden with a sword, Jesus rebuked Him, and among other things, said: "But how then should the scriptures be fulfilled, that it must be so? . . . All this has taken place, that the scriptures of the prophets might be fulfilled" (Matt. 26:54, 56).

Jesus felt that all that God had been doing in history from the beginning was now being consummated in Him. The divine purpose of salvation, which had been carried forward in all God's acts with His people throughout their history, was now to be achieved in Him. The old exodus by which the old Israel had been constituted a people was to be fulfilled in Him in a new and greater exodus by which a new Israel would be constituted to include all nations. The Old Covenant was to find its true meaning in the New Covenant to which Jeremiah had looked forward, written on the tables of men's hearts; the old sacrifices were to be gathered up in the one supreme sacrifice toward which they had been pointing, the sacrifice of Christ on the cross. By a series of profound correspondences, Jesus' whole life became one grand exposition of the entire Old Testament. The one thread binding all the thought and behavior of Jesus together is His supreme awareness that the divine action in the Old Testament was coming to its completion in Him.[7]

This survey of correspondences between the Old Testament and Jesus' awareness that it was being brought to its consummation in Him could be extended at length. At every turn of His life Jesus felt that He was under the control of an eternal purpose which had been working itself out on the stage of history through His people, Israel, and was now to be climaxed in Him. Commenting on this, Hoskyns and Davey have written: "The uniqueness of the obedience of Jesus was dictated by a creative and penetrating insight into the meaning of the Old Testament Scriptures. . . . This was the conscious purpose which lay behind and conditioned His words and actions."[8] "Jesus acted as

He did act and said what He did say because He was
consciously fulfilling a necessity imposed upon Him by
God through the demands of the Old Testament."[9] If the
Old Testament was interwoven into the thought and behavior and obedience of Jesus to this extent, it would seem
that we would neglect it at our peril. If Jesus heard the
voice of God in the Old Testament Scriptures, we shall
too, if we "have ears to hear." And if these Scriptures were
so paramount to Him, how shall we understand Him if we
do not take them into account?

A second major consideration in confirming the worth
of the Old Testament to the Christian church is the fact
that it was the Bible of the New Testament church. A
thorough look at the New Testament indicates that its
writers felt that what God had done for them in Christ was
to be understood in the light of God's action recorded in
the Old Testament. The tremendous dynamic which sent
them out to proclaim their Lord to the whole world could
not, in their minds, be dissociated from the Old Testament. They did not merely preach Jesus—they preached
Jesus as the fulfillment of the Old Testament Scriptures.

This can be plainly seen in the early preaching of the
church as set forth in the Book of the Acts. The very first
words that are recorded on Christian lips after the ascension of Jesus are Peter's words to the gathered one hundred and twenty in the upper room: "Brethren, the scripture had to be fulfilled" (Acts 1:16). Then, in his first
sermon on the day of Pentecost, after a sentence to gain
the attention of the crowd, Peter said, " . . . This is what was
spoken by the prophet Joel," and proceeded to quote at
length from this prophecy (Acts 2:16ff.). Then he added
that the crucifixion of Jesus was "according to the definite
plan and foreknowledge of God," and ended by setting the
Resurrection in relation to certain Old Testament Psalms.
Peter's second recorded sermon at the Beautiful Gate follows a similar pattern. "The God of Abraham and of Isaac
and of Jacob, the God of our fathers, glorified his servant

Jesus," he affirmed (Acts 3:13). Then later he added, "But what God foretold by the mouth of all the prophets, that his Christ should suffer, he thus fulfilled" (Acts 3:18). The rest of the sermon is one clear presentation of the fact that what had happened in Jesus was the establishing of "all that God spoke by the mouth of his holy prophets from of old" (Acts 3:21). When Peter addressed the Sanhedrin after his first arrest, he quoted Psalm 118: "This is the stone which was rejected by you builders, but which has become the head of the corner" (Acts 4:11). Then later, when after his release from prison he joined the others, they prayed together, finding words to express their sense of the meaning of that moment in Psalm 2 (Acts 4:25ff.). There is not room to follow through the whole Book of the Acts—Stephen's address, Peter's rebuke of Simon Magus, Philip's experience with the Ethiopian eunuch, Paul's early preaching in Damascus, Peter's sermon in the home of Cornelius, Paul's sermon at Antioch of Pisidia, the Council of Jerusalem, Paul's preaching at Corinth, the preaching of Apollos at Corinth—to point out that the thinking of the early church was shot through with the Old Testament. The same phenomenon is to be seen in the Gospels and the Epistles. The Old Testament was the Bible of the early church, and a much-used one. Although they knew that Jesus had brought something entirely new into being by His coming, they also recognized that this was in continuity with what God had been doing historically with Israel as depicted in the Old Testament. In pointing us back to the Scriptures of the Old Testament, says Luther, the writers of the New Testament are trying "to teach us that the Scriptures are not to be despised, but diligently read. For they themselves base the New Testament upon them mightily, proving it by the Old Testament and appealing to it. . . . And what is the New Testament but a public preaching and proclamation of Christ, set forth through the sayings of the Old Testament and fulfilled through Christ."[10] Now if the Old Testament was so crucial to the writers of the New Testament, is it not likely that we shall do well to stand with them in this regard, and listen with them for the voice of God?

One further thing. Quite apart from Jesus' evaluation of the Old Testament and that of the early church, it would be impossible to understand the New Testament without the Old. The very name "Jesus Christ" is without meaning apart from the Old Testament. The title really means "Jesus, the Christ." What Christ? Obviously, the Christ of the Old Testament. One must therefore cast a messianic look back over the Jewish Scriptures to give content to the title by which our Lord is described. Likewise, the name "Christian" that we bear needs the Old Testament for its explication, for, as Professor Anders Nygren has reminded us,

> that too builds on the Old Testament. In Acts it is reported that "in Antioch the disciples were for the first time called Christians [christianoi]" (11:26). "Christ" is of course the Greek translation of the Old Testament name "Messiah." The "Christians" are the new messianic congregation, which has received from God the fulfilment of the promises given in the Old Testament; they are the holy people of God gathered around his Messiah.[11]

The Old Testament, therefore, is indispensable to an understanding of our Lord as Messiah—Son of Man—Suffering Servant and equally indispensable to an understanding of ourselves as Christians.

Furthermore, both John the Baptist and Jesus announce the coming of "the kingdom of God," and that phrase is used countless times in the New Testament. Strangely, however, the kingdom is never defined as such. The New Testament seems to proceed on the basis that those who heard this expression in New Testament times knew what it meant. Jesus obviously had to pour new content into the term and redefine it; but what it was He was redefining was evidently well known to His hearers. The kingdom of which both John and Jesus spoke had to be that "reign of God" which the Old Testament promised. We must, therefore, rely on the Old Testament to lend the clues for understanding the kingdom.

It seems clear, then, that the Old Testament is indispensable to the Christian church and that the spiritual instinct which led the early church to combine the Old Testament writings with those of the New Testament into one Bible was an altogether trustworthy one. But granted all this, how is the Old Testament to be related to the New? How is it to be understood in the church? Obviously, there is much in it which is time-conditioned and not permanent, local and not universal, earthen vessel and not treasure. It seems quite plain, for example, that the writers of the Old Testament had a three-storied view of the universe. Need we accept that on the authority of the Old Testament? The Old Testament allowed no usury. Does its authority invalidate the modern system of money-lending at controlled interest rates? The Old Testament countenanced slavery. Does its authority justify slavery today? Do the ceremonial and sacrificial laws of the Old Testament and the Old Testament's designation of the seventh day as the Sabbath bind us today? Do the dietary laws of the Old Testament forbid us to eat pork? What about the rules for testing the guilt of certain criminals, or the land laws, or polygamy, or any number of other features of the Old Testament? They are hardly authoritative over us today. Wherein, then, does the authority of the Old Testament lie? On what is the unity of the Old and New Testaments to be based? How may we tell what is, or is not, of value to the Christian church in the Old Testament?

This is a difficult problem, and certainly not all the ramifications of it can be dealt with here. Details must give way to sketching in the broad outline of an answer. It seems to me that the major clue is to be found in the opening verses of the Letter to the Hebrews. There we read: "God, who at sundry times and in divers manners spake in time past unto the fathers by the prophets, hath in these last days spoken unto us by his Son" (1:1, 2a). Here, among other items, two things stand out clearly. The first is the continuity between the two testaments, with God as the subject of both. *God* spoke in time past unto the fathers by the prophets; also it was *God* who spoke unto us in a Son. The unifying element, that which guarantees continuity between the two testaments, is the fact that the same God speaks in both. But not only is there continuity here; there is also discontinuity. It is evident that the writer believes that God's final speaking in His Son is unique, something entirely new, which goes quite beyond what He had said to the fathers through the prophets in snippets and in metaphors. These two things, then, give us the clue to the interrelationships between the two testaments. Since there is continuity, Christ must be understood in the light of that which led up to Him. Since there is also discontinuity, what led up to Him must have light thrown back on it by Christ. The movement goes both ways. The Old Testament interprets Christ, and Christ interprets the Old Testament. This has been illustrated by the relation of a tidal river to the sea. The river flows into the sea, and the sea backs up into the river. The river is the river, and the sea is the sea; but there is an intermingling of the two and a mutuality of movement between them that makes it impossible to separate them. Each contributes to the other. The Old Testament stream flows on to Christ; Christ, on the other hand, flows back into the Old Testament.

The Gospel writers' intermingling of the ministries of John the Baptist and Jesus makes this plain. At this point they are all at one. Mark begins his Gospel in what would otherwise be a most peculiar way: "The beginning of the gospel of Jesus Christ, the Son of God" (1:1). Then, after quoting a passage from Isaiah, he says: "John the baptizer appeared preaching. . ." (vs. 4). In other words, the ministry of John, climaxing the Old Testament, is the beginning of the ministry of Jesus. Matthew, after telling the stories relating to Jesus' birth, immediately says: "In those days came John the Baptist, preaching . . ." (3:1). Luke outdoes Matthew at this point in that he tells the story of John's birth as well as that of Jesus' birth. But more than that, he tells of the annunciation of John's birth as well as that of Jesus'. The two annunciation stories and the two birth stories are so interwoven that it is plain that in Luke's mind there is also a theological commingling of the two (see Luke 1:5-2:20). It is striking also that the Fourth Gospel, so different from the other three in so many ways, is at one with them in beginning the ministry of Jesus with that of John the Baptist. After the prologue, which was likely written later as a modern writer would write a preface after completing his work, the first sentence in John's story about Jesus reads: "And this is the record of John" (1:19).

How could it have been made clearer by the Gospel writers that they saw an ineradicable relationship between the two testaments in the ministries of John and Jesus. To understand Jesus one must understand John as the Elijah foretold in the Old Testament; and to understand John fully one must see him in the light of Jesus, who brought a kingdom whose least subject is greater than John (Luke 7:28). The authority of both testaments is so closely connected that when Jesus was asked, "By what authority doest thou these things?" He replied: "Was the baptism of John from heaven or from men?" (Luke 20:2, 4). Jesus' authority and that of the Old Testament through John stand or fall together. They are so closely related that either they are both "from heaven" or they are both merely "of men." If they are "from heaven," then they are backed by the authority of the same God. It is God, then, speaking through both testaments, who gives them their unity.

The Christian use of the Old Testament, therefore, is to

listen for the voice of the same God who has spoken in
Jesus Christ. And since the Old Testament is a long conversation of God with His people over more than 1500 years,
the authentic voice of God may be discerned by examining
the writings as a whole so that the authentic lineaments of
His speaking begin to be plain. There is much in the Old
Testament which reflects not the voice of God, but the
faulty human instruments to whom, and through whom,
He spoke. It may be difficult, and in some measure subjective, to try to distinguish between the authentic voice of
God and the voices of the men through whom He worked.
But the effort must be made. Otherwise, we shall miss the
voice of God in the Old Testament and find it of no use, as
we have seen is true with many; or we shall misunderstand
God's voice in the Old Testament by confusing it with
human voices.

Perhaps it would be helpful to recall an illustration I
used earlier. Marcia Davenport, the daughter of the famous
opera singer Alma Gluck, tells us in her recent book *Too
Strong for Fantasy* that one of her most treasured posses-
sions is a set of about 140 of her mother's recordings.
These were made for the "old hand-cranked Victor
machine with the convolvulus-shaped horn, and the slight-
ly newer Victrola without the horn which presently suc-
ceeded it."[12]   Recording methods in those days were
"primitive and orchestral accompaniments, by comparison
with today, laughable." "Her records are almost unobtain-
able and those in existence are more than likely to be
badly worn." But, says her daughter, "If . . . a record of
Alma Gluck's in reasonably good surface condition is
played on a modern phonograph, adjusted to no greater
dynamic amplification than the volume of a normal voice,
it may be understood why for me and for others like me,
there is no present-day *singing* of the same definition."[13]
Obviously, there are extraneous sounds, scratching, click-
ing, distortion. These are not to be confused with the voice
of Alma Gluck; they are merely accompaniments of it. But

in spite of these, the voice is recognizable and unmistakably hers, and carries that almost unique quality which was "the result of a combination of natural equipment with the self-application of standards of technique which no longer exist."[14] Many true connoisseurs of music would prefer to hear Alma Gluck's voice on a poor record than most voices in our time on virtually flawless records.

Does this help us understand the relation of the Old Testament to the voice of God? The human instruments to whom He spoke and through whom He speaks to us were imperfect. There may be much accompanying His voice that is extraneous, diverting, distorting. But through the distortion sounds the authentic voice, the voice of the same God who spoke His final word through a perfect instrument in whom there was no distortion, His Son. The voice is discernible by those who love it. And as Jesus said in another connection, ". . . The sheep follow him, for they know his voice. . . . They know not the voice of strangers" (John 10:4, 5). In spite of all the difficulties in the Old Testament, I am convinced that it is a sufficiently clear medium of the voice of God that a questing soul who goes there in search of God will find Him. One does not have to be expert in dealing with all the fine points of Old Testament criticism to hear God's voice there. This is not to say that these fine points are not necessary for the church's total understanding of the Old Testament, nor that without a knowledge of them we may sometimes arrive at misunderstandings. But enough comes through without this knowledge to live and die by. And if Sir W. Robertson Nicoll was right in affirming that in the soul's quest for God "the indispensable conditions of insight" are "humility, and pain, and need, and soul travail, and a pure intent,"[15] it may be that at times the voice of God comes through more authentically to the humble, untutored seeker than to the learned.

Few, perhaps, are the learned that will admit this. One such, however, who was one of the most learned men I have ever known, Dr. George W. Richards, used to tell of playing in the yard as a little boy and seeing in the window his old grandmother sitting in her rocking chair reading her Bible. She, he insisted, at many points knew what that Bible meant far better than the scholars. And if I may add my own word, after dealing with the study of the Bible at a professional level for most of a lifetime, I still know that at certain points I do not hear the voice of God through it as clearly as my own mother did, whose critical knowledge was minimal. Knowledge is good, but as II Peter suggests, we need to add to our "knowledge temperance; and to temperance patience; and to patience godliness; and to godliness brotherly kindness; and to brotherly kindness charity. For if these things be in you, and abound, they make you that ye shall neither be barren nor unfruitful in the knowledge of our Lord Jesus Christ. But he that lacketh these things is blind . . ." (1:6-9, NEB). As Forsyth once said, "the Bible's real value" comes through "realizing the experience of its grace."[16] Read the Old Testament in this light, and it will authenticate itself as the instrument of God's voice to us, whose continuity with the New Testament lies in the one God who in both testaments speaks His word of reconciling grace. The Old Testament will shed its light on the New by depicting the one "long divine act" beginning with Abraham and culminating in Jesus Christ, which entire act is the story of our redemption. Particular problems may still perplex us, but the redemptive thread running through the whole will be a sure guide to our Redeemer. As Forsyth put it, ". . . We may not feel compelled to take the whole Bible, but we must take the Bible as a whole."[17] There are different levels of discourse in the Bible. "The Lord is my shepherd," for example, or "God is our refuge and strength, a very present help in trouble" speak to us at a different level than descriptions of Jerusalem's water supply, or the fact that Buz was the brother of Uz! When you read the Old Testament, then, do not stumble over problems. Let them await further light while you search through and beyond them for your Redeemer. Look for the continuity of the Old Testament with the New, for those signposts pointing you to Christ.

But the New Testament is also discontinuous with the Old. This does not divide them, but rightly understood binds them even closer together, for that which is unique in the New Testament casts its light back on the Old Testament. To repeat a metaphor we used earlier, if the Old Testament is the river flowing into the New, the New Testament is the sea backing up into the river. Christ gives a meaning to the Old Testament which it cannot have apart from Him. This leads us to the very difficult problem of the Christological interpretation of the Old Testament—how properly to interpret the Old Testament in the light of its fulfillment in Jesus Christ. This is a much debated question today. The issue is put clearly by a Swedish scholar, Olof Linton:

> Luther looked at the entire Bible from the viewpoint of the gospel and of faith in Christ; that which came later shed its light on what had gone before. But the newer research has rejected that principle. For the interpretation of a text appeal may be made only to contemporary and earlier texts. . . . The interpretation of the Old Testament is freed from New Testament concepts. . . . Each text must speak for itself.[18]

If this is true, then Christ does not shed light on our understanding of the Old Testament. It may be studied only in the light of what it meant to the men who wrote it at the time it was written. The study of the Old Testament is a purely historical study, not a theological study; or, in so far as it is a theological study, it is a search only for the theology of the Old Testament Jews, and not *Christian* theology.

But do we Christians find in the Old Testament only what the first-century or eighth-century B.C. Jews found? Or, for that matter, what a contemporary Jew may find

there? Some years ago, I heard a discussion between Su-
zanne de Dietrich, a remarkable French lay theologian, and
an outstanding Old Testament scholar. Miss de Dietrich
was insisting on understanding the Old Testament in some
sense through Christ. The Old Testament scholar was hold-
ing out for a purely historical, non-Christological understanding. Finally, she protested, in her vigorous, high-
pitched voice: "Well, we are not Jews. We are Christians!
We do not read the Old Testament as Jews; we read it as
Christians!" Which view was right? Certainly Paul and
Luther would have been on the side of seeing the Old
Testament in the light of Christ. Were they wrong?

Paul insisted that something absolutely new, something
unique, had happened in Christ which changed everything.
It changed our standing with God, and changed our whole
understanding of what God was doing in the events recorded in the Old Testament. Paul insisted that apart from
Christ, "whenever Moses is read a veil lies over their minds;
but when a man turns to the Lord the veil is removed" (II
Cor. 3:15-16). He also said that "the mystery, which was
kept secret since the world began . . . now is made manifest" through "the preaching of Jesus Christ." But, he
added, this open secret is now "made known to all nations
for the obedience of faith" through "the scriptures of the
prophets" (Rom. 16:25, 26). These passages seem to suggest that Christ had removed a veil and enabled men to see
a hidden mystery in the scriptures of the prophets which
could not be seen before. The writer to the Hebrews tells
us that all the Old Testament worthies "died in faith, not
having received the promises, but having seen them afar
off" (11:13). When what they embraced from a distance
finally became manifest, is it true interpretation to see in
their faith only that which they then saw, or to see in it
what it finally came to mean when the promise was fulfilled?

The clue to understanding here may lie in a distinction
between what the ancient prophet said and what *God* was

saying through him. It may well be that God had more to say through the prophets than they themselves were aware. It is characteristic of all works of inspiration that they often transcend the "conscious horizon of the artist."[19] To limit the meaning of their work to their own intention, therefore, may severely curtail their worth. In a remarkable study of the work of Charles Williams on Dante, Dorothy Sayers makes this principle clear:

> A poet creates a character, a situation, a phrase for a particular purpose, and *after* having done so, realizes that he has created a universal symbol, applicable in a far wider sense than that which he immediately intended. . . . But it sometimes happens that it is not the poet himself, but another, who discovers the wider relevance. If so, he is justified in so interpreting in the place where he finds it; for the relevance was always potentially there, and once seen and recognized it is actually there for ever. This does not, of course, mean that we can "read into" poets anything that we jolly well like; any significance that contradicts the whole tenor of their work is obviously suspect. But it means that in a very real sense poets do sometimes write more greatly than they know.[20]

The principle involved here is that "in the tradition—which means the 'handing over'—of the symbols of art, time's arrow flies both ways. That which was always potentially in the earlier poet may be actualized in the later poet, and, once it has been actualized it becomes and remains actual in the poet of its origin."[21] In other words, what Williams saw in Dante was something no one before, not even Dante, had seen. But if he really saw it, if it was really there, it was there whether Dante consciously intended it or not. Williams made his contribution to Dante, as Dante made his contribution to Williams.

Another example of this principle is to be seen in an exchange P. T. Forsyth had with the English artist George Frederick Watts. Forsyth was giving a series of lectures on "Religion in Recent Art." In interpreting one of Watts' paintings, he suddenly thought he saw something in it which was not obvious on the surface but which struck him with great force. He was reluctant to offer his interpretation, however, lest he should be seeing in Watts' painting what the artist had not put there. He was never able to question Watts directly on the matter but he did receive an answer through Watts' wife. The artist indicated that what Forsyth had seen in his painting had never so much as entered his mind. But now that Forsyth had pointed it out, he himself saw that it was there. His genius had put more into the picture than he had consciously intended. In other words, Forsyth made his contribution to Watts, as Watts had made his contribution to Forsyth. The movement was both ways.

The application of this to the Old Testament is that Christ made His contribution to the understanding of the Old Testament. He made actual what was there only potentially before. Now that the potential has been made actual, it remains actual forever.

This does not mean, of course, that we are free to do what some do in trying to read Christian meanings into the Old Testament—engage in a process similar to lying on our backs and watching the clouds, seeing in them whatever elephants or giraffes or castles or faces our imaginations suggest to us. Forsyth cautioned that "we must indeed avoid and reprobate interpretations which are as alien to [the original] intention as the chief baker's three baskets are to the doctrine of the Trinity, or the 'badgers' skins dyed red,' in Exodus, are to the atonement. But," he added, "while we refuse to do violence to the text, we must equally refuse to go no further than itself on its own road."[22] The words "on its own road" are the important ones here. We must do no violence to the intention of the original writer. But to allow the Old Testament writer to set us on his road, then to travel that road further in the light of Christ, in a direction that is "really and reasonably congruous" with his "central idea," is entirely legitimate.

The important thing, therefore, is not just what an Old

Testament writer meant—though that is important and indispensable—but what God meant to say through him; and that we now see in Jesus Christ. Thus the approach to the Old Testament for purely historical purposes, and the approach to it for the purposes of Christian theology, are both valid—but the latter must finally command the former. It is important to know what God said to His ancient people. It is more important to know what He was finally intending to say at a deeper level in Jesus Christ. The two meanings are not contradictory; the second merely deepens the first.

Suppose, for example, you take the response of a learned scientist to a question asked by his five-year-old child. It would make no sense at all to the child if the father replied in terms of his own total knowledge. A wise father will give an answer which may not be technically nor totally true, but which is the best that can be done to express truth within the limits of the child's capacity to take it in. Later, when the child is grown up, the father can tell him much that could not be said earlier. The fuller answer will be consonant with the earlier, but will take the question much further than the earlier answer could. When the full and final answer comes, it does not contradict what was said earlier, but throws light back on the earlier reply and fills it with meaning.

When a play is written, there may be aspects of the early scenes which are not plain as one reads or sees it. Or they may be quite plain but seemingly not very significant to the plot. But when the climax of the play is reached, immediately the earlier confusion is cleared up or the insignificant leaps into profound significance. The author of the play, knowing the total sweep of it and where it was coming out, wove into the earlier scenes things which could not at that time be made plain. The significance of those scenes is not to be seen in what they mean to the reader as he reads them for the first time, but in what they mean in the light of the final outcome.

Many years ago, a Michigan farmer made a pact with his son that if he would follow certain behavior patterns until he was twenty-one years of age, he would give him a horse and buggy. The lad made good in keeping his end of the bargain. The twenty-first birthday arrived, and it was time to fulfil the promise. In the meantime, Henry Ford had been tinkering around in Detroit, and automobiles had come in. The last thing the boy now wanted was a horse and buggy. The father, knowing that the intention of his promise could no longer be fulfilled with a horse and buggy, wisely gave his son a car. Now let us suppose that the father had had foreknowledge that cars were to be available when his son's twenty-first birthday came, and had told the son, "When you are twenty-one, I will give you a horseless carriage." The boy, never having heard of such, much less having seen one, would have found such a promise mystifying. Even if the father had known that cars were to be available when his son was twenty-one, he still would have had to promise him a horse and buggy to give the promise meaning to the son when it was made. By that promise, however, he would have had more in mind than the form of the promise at that time could intelligibly carry.

In some such fashion as this, we can see how God intended more through what He said to the prophets than their words at first conveyed. God had Christ in mind all the time, but the mystery could not be cleared up until Christ came. When, therefore, Paul and Luther read Christian meanings into the Old Testament, they were not stupidly suggesting that this is what the Old Testament writers meant. They were saying that this is the deeper meaning that God had in mind. Luther makes this plain. Speaking about Paul's use of Deuteronomy 30:12 in Romans 10, he says: "Moses did not use this word with that intention. But the apostle, with his unsurpassably clear and spirit-filled insight, sets forth the very core of its meaning; for he shows us that Scripture everywhere speaks only of

Christ, if one looks deeply."[23] Thus Luther, as Professor Nygren says,

> understands very well that Paul is not attempting to set forth the simple, historical significance of a scriptural statement; but he is just as sure that Paul has set forth God's ultimate meaning, when the apostle views God's preparatory revelation in the light of his full revelation in Christ. . . . His purpose is not to trace the literal, human meaning of the words. He asks what *God means to say to us* through them. And yet he does not allow himself to interpret them any way he pleases. God himself, by his new action in Christ, has interpreted his Old Testament word.[24]

The Old Testament, therefore, is definitely an indispensable part of the Christian Scriptures. We need it to help us understand Christ. On the other hand, we need Him to help us understand the Old Testament. It is in this mutuality, this combination of continuity and discontinuity set forth in Hebrews 1:1, 2, that the relationship of the two testaments is to be seen.

Chapter Four

The Authority of the Bible Over Christian Experience

With regard to the Christian faith, personal experience is at once the most vital and the most problematic, the most solid and the most ephemeral, the most necessary and the most untrustworthy, part of life. Christianity is nothing if it is not a profoundly experienced reality, a personal confrontation by and surrender to the Creator and Lord of life, who says to us: "I have called you by name, you are mine" (Isa. 43:1). In this it differs from other religions and from philosophies. Professor Paul Shorey, perhaps the most eminent authority on Plato in his day, "once said that a man might be a good Platonist though he had never read a line of Plato or had never even heard of him, because Plato's ideas flowed through so many streams from their source in Plato's writings."[1] This could not be true of Christ. No man can be a Christian if he has never been personally confronted by Christ, no matter how many Christian ideas have filtered through to him from many streams. To be a Christian is to "know" Christ in the deep sense of personal trust in and commitment to Him, of intimate communion with Him, and of at least a desire to obey His will.

But having said this, we must also recognize that all sorts of aberrations have been passed off in the name of Christian experience, and many have stumbled or fallen from the faith through trusting subjective experiences which had no substance and turned out to be sheer fancy. Paul staked his apostleship and his eternal hope on the reality of his experience with the risen Lord on the road to Damascus. Yet he raised questions with some in the Corinthian church who were molding the faith around so-called "spiritual" experiences, and insisted that however much a man "thinks that he is . . . spiritual," he was yet to subject his own experiences to apostolic authority as "a command of the Lord" (I Cor. 14:37).

The theme suggested by this two-sided emphasis is that although Christian experience is necessary and desirable, it is never a safe guide in measuring the faith. Experience can never be the criterion of worth or meaning, but must always be subjected to the Word of God in the Scriptures. The gospel contained in the Scriptures should evoke genuine experience, but the thing experienced is more important than the experience. Or, to put it more correctly from the standpoint of the Christian faith, He who is experienced—God in Christ—is more important than he who experiences. The ultimate goal of the Christian faith is not to produce states of mind, or ecstasies of feeling, or mystic experiences. It is rather that "in everything God may be glorified through Jesus Christ" (I Pet. 4:11). It is well that we be able to say with the healed blind man in John 9, "One thing I know, that though I was blind, now I see" (vs. 25). This, no one could take away from him. But the major issue in this passage was not his experience of seeing, but who it was who made him whole. Was this one of "the works of God"? (vs. 3). Was He who did this work "the light of the world"? (vs. 5). Was He "from God"? (vss. 16, 33). Was He a mere "prophet"? (vs. 17). "Where" was the source of His power? (vss. 29, 30). Was He "the Son of man"? (vs. 35). The center of the whole story was not that a blind man experienced sight. The real issue was, Who is the One who produced the experience? The climax is reached when the one who had the experience turned away from his experience to the One who had healed him, and said, "Lord, I believe," and worshiped Him (vs. 38). Without the focus on the One who did the healing, the experience of healing would merely have placed the blind man in the state of the others around him who had eyes but were "blind" to who Jesus was, and remained in their sins (vss. 39, 41).

Let us now look at the limitations of experience as a guide in matters of the faith. First, experience is too subjective. It may have no validity at all. It may be merely a state of mind, without reality, without value. It may have no more worth than a drug trip. These trips take one away from the world of reality into the realm of fantasy. The participant has experiences, but they are all in his own mind—there is no objective fact producing the experience or corresponding to what is felt. It is purely an inner state with no content which can be communicated to others, and one which functions for the person experiencing it only to the degree that he is removed from himself. It is merely a temporary escape from one's self, which ulti- mately damages the ego and makes it impossible for one to be fully a person. Religious experiences could have the same effect. They could be temporary escapes into a world of euphoria, emotional binges subjectively induced, with nothing of God in them.

Christianity is a "historical" religion, a religion which purports to confront us with external, objective facts, what God did "for us men and for our salvation." The reality of it depends wholly on God who saves us rather than on our feelings of being saved. It is conceivable that one could "feel" saved and not be so. On the other hand it is also conceivable that one could have no "feeling" of being saved, and still be so. As an illustration, consider a man who takes a drug and who then goes swimming, gets beyond his depth, and drowns. It is possible that the effect of the drug would be such that as he went down for the last time he would have the euphoric sensation of some- one's rescuing him, or perhaps an even higher feeling of security, as though he were floating off into a world of heavenly bliss. Feeling or no feeling, he would drown. On the other hand, take a person who with all his powers at his command gets into trouble in the water. After a long struggle, he goes down for the last time and is suffocated into unconsciousness. At that point, a strong swimmer arrives, pulls him from the waves, administers artificial respiration, and brings him back to consciousness. With the "feeling" of drowning, and then finally with no "feeling" at all, the victim is saved. The real point at issue in a potential drowning situation has nothing to do with the subjective state of the victim. It has everything to do with objective realities outside the victim and whether they are early enough and strong enough to effect a rescue. So it is with the Christian faith. The important thing is not whether I "feel" saved, but whether God's saving deeds in Jesus Christ are mighty enough to take care of the needs of my soul. The significant thing is not my emotional state, but whether He is "mighty to save and strong to deliver."

In his recent work *The Judgment of Jonah,* Jacques Ellul has written some wise words in this regard:

> When we try to build on our spiritual experiences, on the facts in our lives which we see to be of God, we oscillate . . . between joy and doubt, for we are never certain of what we have lived through or of the interpretation we have given it . . . . All the uncertainties which might result from subjective experiences disappear if instead of stopping at them we refer them to God, if it is God who counts and not our experiences. . . . Why be shattered . . . when the sigh gives place to the reality? . . . To refer all to God, to count on God's patience and love, to respect his freedom, to love his will—all this objectivity sometimes leaves us cold when we ought to be reassured by it and confident, since we are placing our very doubts on certainty.[2]

One is also impressed with the wisdom of John Wesley in his dealings with men at this point (as in many others!). As is well known, Wesley's ministry produced highly emotional states. People went into trances, were physically convulsed, were seized by fits of sobbing, gave out loud cries, or went into periods of longer or shorter emotional depression and distress. One might think, therefore, that Wesley put store by such experiences and used them to authenticate his work. This, however, is not so. It is true that he carefully examined his own states of mind and made careful studies of the emotional reactions of many others. He did want to experience the Christian faith, and he did want others to be led to a genuine experience of Christ. He even validated some of his views by gathering a sufficiently broad number of confirming experiences to convince him that such a multitude of sincere people could hardly be wrong. But even Wesley would not have trusted any subjective experiences that he could not be convinced were produced by the objective working of the Spirit of God, and which could not be authenticated by the objective "good news" contained in the Scriptures.

In his *Journal*, he makes the following entry:

> At Weavers' Hall I . . . earnestly exhorted all that followed after holiness to avoid, as fire, all who do not speak according "to the Law and Testimony." In the afternoon I preached at the Fishponds, but had no life or spirit in me, and was much in doubt whether God would not lay me aside and send other labourers into His harvest. I came to the society full of this thought; and began, in much weakness, to explain, "Beloved, believe not every spirit, but try the spirits, whether they be of God." I told them they were not to judge of the spirit whereby any one spoke either by appearances, or by common report, or by their own inward feelings. No, nor by any dreams, visions, or revelations supposed to be made to their souls; any more than by their tears, or any involuntary effects wrought upon their bodies. I warned them all these were, in themselves, of a doubtful, disputable nature; they might be from God, and they might not; and were therefore not simply to be relied on (any more than simply to be condemned), but to be tried by a farther rule to be brought to the only certain test—the Law and the Testimony.[3]

What could be clearer than that Wesley was interested not in inducing states of mind or religious experiences, but in squaring men's lives with "the Law and the Testimony"— the Scriptures?

Anders Nygren makes the same point: "When one people, engaged in mortal combat with another, receives a message from the latter offering peace, what is crucial is not their feelings and subjective state, but the terms which the message actually proposes. It is the same with the Bible. When God sends his message to us, when he offers us a covenant of peace, our prime business is to listen to what he says to us."[4] Hence, to "tell people how they ought to feel towards Christ . . . is useless. It is just what they ought that they cannot do." The important thing is, "What has God said or done for my soul." The focus should be on the "Christ that will make [men] feel as they ought."[5]

A second limitation of experience as a guide in matters of faith is that it is too individualistic. Our own experience is necessarily private, detached, isolated, whereas the Christian faith is corporate and communal. It is true, as we have seen in an earlier chapter, that genuine authority over us is spiritual authority, that authority which authenticates itself and is therefore freely and inwardly accepted by those over whom it is exercised. And for this reason, the rights of the private conscience must be guarded and a certain measure of inward liberty of judgment maintained. Furthermore, the Christian faith is highly personal. My faith must be *my* faith. "The God of Abraham, and the God of Isaac, and the God of Jacob" (Matt. 22:32), "the God and Father of our Lord Jesus Christ" (II Cor. 1:3), must become *my* God. No one else can live my life, and certainly no one else can die my death. At the center of a number of concentric circles, including humanity, my nation, my community, and my family, there is finally my own personhood where, in spite of all my relationships and of the influence these have on me, I am *I*. And just as my death is a highly personal experience which no one else can share, so my faith must be my own.

But this personalizing of the faith must never lead to an individualism which isolates my faith from the family of believers, or sets up my private judgment in a way that isolates me from the corporate judgment of the church. For we are not individual Christians, we are members of a body. "And the spirits of prophets are subject to prophets" (I Cor. 14:32). My individuality must be controlled by the group, the church. In trying to correct those in the church in Corinth who claimed to have had "spiritual" experiences of their own which were authoritative over them and gave them authority over others, Paul reminded them that "as the body is one and has many members, and all the members of the body, though many, are one body, so it is with Christ" (I Cor. 12:12). If, therefore, any one member forgets his membership in the whole body, and exalts himself and his experiences as though he were the whole, this would be as ridiculous as the eye saying that it was "the whole body" (I Cor. 12:17). No, says Paul, each one is a "member in particular" of the entire "body of Christ" (I Cor. 12:27, KJV). He must, therefore, function as a member of the body, and not as an isolated individual.

As Christians, we are social beings. In the words of H. Scott Holland, "Our inward freedom belongs to us, not in our own name, . . . our liberty is an exercise of a common right, which we share with others, who are one with us in the body. . . . These powers are drawn out of the common heritage. They are the expression of a common energy. They . . . move towards a common end. We are free only so far as we are the organ of this common life."[6] We are, therefore, under the authority of "this inherited story into which we have been born."[7] Our private experiences must be put to the test of the total experience of the whole church. Our individuality must be subject to a larger authority than our own.

This raises a problem, of course, which can be hazardous

in another direction if not properly understood. If my individual experience is under the authority of the corporate experience of the church, is the church always right and am I always wrong? A great deal is made of this today, where the voice of the courts of the church is frequently declared to be the voice of God. Much of the political maneuvering that goes on behind the scenes, in committees, in private quarters, over dinner tables, to swing the church in a direction already decided as good by those in the power structure, is presented to the public as the voice of the Holy Spirit. Now since God uses "the wrath of man" to His own praise, it is also possible that at times the outcome of sheer political power in the church may be the voice of the Holy Spirit. On the other hand, we are told in the Book of the Revelation that the best that our Lord can do at times is to "stand at the door [of the church] and knock" (3:20). I am not sure that He always gets in. If the voice of the church at any moment is always the voice of God, then Luther was wrong when he stood alone at the Diet of Worms against church, pope, Fathers, and councils. If, on the other hand, the Reformation he began was worthy, and has lived to release the power of the gospel in men's lives, Luther was right. This one instance suggests that there are times when the corporate church, or any particular group of Christian people gathered at any particular occasion, may be wrong. The truth is not to be determined by counting ecclesiastical noses following some clever manipulation, or by the mass psychology of applause, or by the creation of a mood where intelligent dissent is discouraged. And it is possible that one man may be the bearer of the truth against a thousand, or ten thousand, people gathered in ecclesiastical conclave. He may be right in saying to the whole ecclesiastical world: "Stand thou on that side, for on this am I!"[8]

Does this not argue, then, against what we have been saying above? Does it not suggest that an individual, apart from his membership in the body, may have an authority greater than the body? It may, on the surface, look so; but in reality it does not. Luther was not standing against the church of his day on the basis of his experience. True, he had had a tremendous experience of release through the gospel. He tells us that when the meaning of Romans 1:17 dawned upon him it was as though he had "entered through open doors into paradise itself."[9] But it was not his subjective experience on which he stood. He staked everything on the objective truth of the Word of God which brought him this experience. He came to this through a process of exegetical study, through long pondering the written Word, through wrestling hard with language. He suddenly discovered that the phrase "the righteousness of God" did not mean a subjective righteousness which he, by his good works, was to attain. It was a wholly objective righteousness, that righteousness which God possesses and gives to men by faith. It was the objective Word of God, therefore, which brought him release. And it was on this Word, not his experience, that Luther stood at the Diet of Worms.

This takes us back to an earlier chapter, where we argued that it is the Word of God which is authoritative over the life of the church. Even the total experience of the church must be subject to the record of the saving events which are normative, not to the subsequent experience of any particular generation of Christians. Luther made much of this in discussing a famous statement of Augustine, who said, in writing against the Manichaeans, "I should not believe the gospel if I did not believe the church."[10] Luther argued that, properly understood in its context, Augustine meant that "the authority of all Christendom" which "throughout the world . . . preaches with one accord the gospel" is sufficient evidence to correct the errors of the Manichaeans.[11] Augustine was using this argument, therefore, as an "external proof" which "can be given to heretics" to show "that it is not their doctrine which is right, but [the] doctrine which all the [Christian] world has with one accord accepted."[12] Augustine would not, Luther argued, have used the authority of the church to convince himself of the truth of the faith. That "would be false and un-Christian. Everyone must believe only because it is the word of God, and because he is convinced in his heart that it is true; even though an angel from heaven and all the world preached to the contrary."[13] And, Luther added, if Augustine's statement cannot "be understood in terms of the external proof of faith by which heretics are refuted . . . then it is better to reject the statement."[14]

Luther saw clearly that the gospel may not be put at the mercy of experience, even if it is the experience of the whole church at any particular time. It is the Scriptures that are the normative record of what the faith is and is not, and they must be authoritative over all subjective experience, whether it be individual or corporate.

A third limitation of Christian experience is that it is too restricted. I cannot allow the gospel to become simply my experience of it without woefully restricting and compressing the gospel. At this point it may be well to try to correct a misapprehension which is often fostered in the name of Paul. Did not Paul rest the gospel on his experience? And did not he get the content of his preaching through his experience on the road to Damascus? The writer of the Acts certainly details that experience in reporting it in Chapter 9, and Paul himself recalls it in some detail in his defense before the mob in Jerusalem in Acts 22, and before Festus and King Agrippa in Acts 26. But does Paul's example in these cases really suggest that his gospel was his experience of the gospel? And is his approach here a pattern for us to follow?

In reply, it should be noted, in the first place, that Paul was not speaking on these occasions about the normal Christian experience which is open to us all. He was speaking of a special post-Resurrection appearance of our Lord to him—an appearance which never ceased to provoke his wonder since it came to him not between the

Resurrection and Ascension of Jesus, as did the post-Resurrection appearances to others, but as a special appearance, "as to one untimely born" (I Cor. 15:8). He indicates that this appearance was the last in a series, after which there were to be no others (I Cor. 15:8). The uniqueness of this confrontation by the risen Lord, then, sets this off from any religious experience possible to us.

Furthermore, Paul used this experience to justify His apostleship, which was vigorously attacked because he had not been one of the original disciples. His apostleship was genuine, he insisted, for he, like the other apostles, had actually seen the risen Lord. It was his apostolic authority, then, which he was vindicating by recounting this experience. It was his apostleship to the uncircumcision, alongside Peter's apostleship to the circumcision, for which he was contending. And it was this experience which gave him apostolic authority to withstand Peter and Barnabas and the others when they sought to restrict the gospel to the Jews. But Paul's gospel was not his experience. It was rather "Jesus Christ . . . publicly portrayed as crucified" (Gal. 3:1). It came from "the scripture" which "preached the gospel beforehand to Abraham" (Gal. 3:8). And when Paul defined to the Christians at Corinth the "gospel which he preached . . . which [they] received . . . by which [they were] saved" (I Cor. 15:1, 2), it was the objective gospel which he had "received" from the apostles who had been with Christ in the flesh, "that Christ died for our sins in accordance with the scriptures, that he was buried, that he was raised on the third day in accordance with the scriptures, and that he appeared to Cephas, then to the twelve," then "to more than five hundred brethren at one time" (I Cor. 15:3-6). He further states that rather than preaching his own experience, he is preaching just what the others were preaching, for he says, "Whether then it was I or they, so we preach and so you believed" (I Cor. 15:11). Paul's gospel was the gospel of the total church, the kerygma announced by all the apostles and believed in the entire church, which went far beyond the limits of his own restricted experience.

There is much about the gospel which one cannot individually experience. We cannot, for example, experience the preexistence of Christ. We cannot experience His sitting "at the right hand of God" (Acts 2:33). We have not seen the risen Jesus, as did Paul and the other apostles. We witness to a Savior who is the Savior of the world, but we cannot experience a "world salvation."[15] Our experience is limited to time and space, but eternity enters us in Christ, "thereby pointing to a Christ larger than our experience. In him we trust but do not experience our own eternity," says Forsyth.[16] Also, the faith we profess and possess is the common faith of the church over the centuries, a church of which "we are but one of many. Therefore Christ, in the common faith of the Church witnesses to himself as transcending our individual experience of him."[17] For these reasons, we dare not limit the gospel to our experience of it.

A fourth limitation of experience is that it is presumptuous and arrogant. If we limit the faith to our experience of it, then we become the criterion by which it is judged and in pride lift ourselves above the gospel itself. If there is that in the faith which I have not experienced, then I am in danger of concluding that it is not the faith. This can lead to a proud disregard for some of the deepest aspects of the faith. As David Paton said some years ago, ". . . So much impoverishment is due to the premature discarding of ancient Christian terms which we have not understood and have therefore thought to be without meaning or truth. We do better to live with them till they yield their meaning."[18] Karl Barth furnishes a good example of the humble waiting that may be necessary to grasp elements of the faith which lie quite beyond one's own subjective experience. Barth, in his early days, had difficulty with the Virgin Birth. In the Swiss Church, the Apostles' Creed is usually recited only on communion Sundays, and is recited by the minister alone. Some ministers who, like Barth, had difficulty with the Virgin Birth simply omitted the phrase "born of the Virgin Mary" from the Creed when they recited it. Barth, however, felt that he was not free to do this. He felt that since this was a part of the faith of the historic church he could not proudly put that faith at the mercy of his own subjectivity. He therefore left it in the Creed when he recited it. Later, after long study and profound struggle, he was able to make that part of the church's faith his own. Is not this attitude better than the presumptive arrogance which proudly constricts the faith to one's own limited experience? Anders Nygren has suggested that "man shows God small honor when he is more interested in his own subjective state than in what God says."[19]

A fifth limitation of experience is that it is too manifold to have any final authority for anybody. Pentecostalism claims to rest on experience. Modern tongues movements and healing movements vindicate themselves by experience. Christian Science rests on experience. Where shall the end be? If private experience is the final authority in the field of the faith, then there is no final authority, and every man will end up doing that which is right in his own eyes. This sort of authority is not only personal, but private. Even where it elicits group assent, it tends finally toward the disintegration of the group into proliferated splinter groups, each of whose special twist of experience demands autonomy. Granted that through the generations there have been wide differences of opinion among those who claim to accept the Scriptures as the final authority for faith, there is in this view at least the hope of some objective control of both private experience and group experience through the solid study of the medium of authority—the Bible.

In recent years, where the study of the Bible by proper exegetical methods has been taken seriously there has been surprising agreement on the meaning of the Scriptures. A study conference was held in Oxford, England, in 1949, including representatives of the Orthodox and Anglican Churches and nearly all branches of Protestantism. The group centered its attention on a specific passage of Scripture. The outcome was amazing, according to participants. At the conclusion of the conference, a "general consensus" was reached, which included the following statement: "It is agreed that the Bible is our common starting point. . . . It is agreed that although we may differ in the manner in which tradition, reason and natural law may be used in the interpretation of Scripture, any teaching that clearly contradicts the biblical position cannot be accepted as Christian."[20] Since then, Roman Catholic scholars have joined in common study of the Scriptures, with similar results. This suggests that to nearly all brands of Christendom today, if the Bible is not the *sole* authority in Christian matters, it is at least the *supreme* authority. The Bible is the common starting point; it is the final court of appeal. This convergence of judgment on the Scriptures from various diverse traditions suggests that the hope for unity in the church is far stronger if the objective authority of the Bible is set above the subjective authority of Christian experience.

One further limitation of experience as authority lies in the fact that its subjectivity is too self-centered and introspective to be spiritually healthy. If Christian experience is to be the final court of appeal in matters of faith, then perforce the focus of religious attention must be within rather than without. The search for security and certainty becomes introspective and psychological. The understanding of the faith becomes self-understanding. The truth about God becomes the truth about man; or to put it perhaps more accurately, the truth about man becomes the truth about God. Theology becomes anthropology. Revelation becomes self-discovery. The search for salvation becomes the effort to "know thyself," in contrast to the biblical insight that "this is eternal life, that [men] know

. . . the only true God, and Jesus Christ whom [he has] sent" (John 17:3). In spite of the fact that this approach has behind it the weight of such a prominent name as that of Rudolf Bultmann, it is highly questionable whether it is a valid one. It could well be that the chaos in the theological world today is at least in part attributable to the subjectivity involved in this approach.

John Wesley's treatment of his own state of mind on the occasion referred to earlier in this chapter is to me very interesting and instructive. When he said that he "had no life or spirit" and that he was "much in doubt whether God would not lay [him] aside and send other labourers into His harvest"—how did he handle this depressing mood? He did not begin to look inside to examine the source of his mood or to find a corrective for it. He went right on with his work, convinced that emotional states of mind were immaterial, and rested his own salvation and the future of his work on "the Law and the Testimony." His own, and other people's, experiences were always to be subjected to the objective Word of God. The central fact of the Christian faith, the fact of being forgiven for sins through Jesus Christ, the fact of being in a justified relation to God, does not rest on experience but on God. As H. B. Swete has put it, "Forgiveness is an act of God which may or may not be followed immediately by a sense of relief. . . . The consciousness of being forgiven is not invariably a result of justification. . . . Forgiveness is necessary to our salvation; the sense of being forgiven is not."[21]

We can never know ourselves sufficiently well to rest our assurance of right relations with God on our own experience. We are a bundle of contradictions. Our sins have marred our self-understanding. Even the most expert psychologist is a warped human being, working with warped tools, on other warped human beings. He may be able to delineate some facets of how warped human beings react to certain situations. He can never, however, so trace the lineaments of the soul that we may rest on this analysis for our spiritual security. Man remains a contradiction, a mystery, to himself. He will never fully know himself. This is unimportant. The significant thing is that he is known by Another, by God, whose knowledge is total and whose wisdom is infinite. As it is stated in I John, even if "our hearts condemn us . . . God is greater than our hearts, and he knows everything" (I John 3:20). "It is better," said P. T. Forsyth, "and safer to pray over the Bible than to brood over self. . . . What really searches us is neither our own introspection, nor God's law, but it is God's Gospel, as it pierces us from the merciless mercy of the Cross and the Son unspared for us."[22] Much spiritual introspection is like blowing our own breath into our own nostrils. It is like artificial respiration administered to ourselves. What we need is the oxygen of the gospel breathed into our spirits from without. Man becomes a living soul not by his own breath but as God breathes into him the breath of life!

Experience in itself is too subjective, too inner, too changeable, too fleeting, too tied to physiological and psychological factors to be a trustworthy guide for faith. To trust our experience is to put our faith at the mercy of our liver, or our endocrine glands, or the quality of our sleep on any given night, or the state of our digestion, or the state of mind of other members of the family, or the problems of our work. Experience must always be subjected to the authority of the saving work of God in Jesus Christ set forth in the Bible. It is *He who saves* who is important, not the feelings of those who are saved. Spiritual health depends on keeping our gaze fixed not on ourselves, but on Him who is "the pioneer and perfecter of our faith" (Heb. 12:2). Augustus Hare insists that the great truth presented by the apostles, and rediscovered by Luther, was

> that we are not to spend our days in watching our own vices, in gazing at our own sins, in stirring and raking up all the mud

of our past lives; but to lift our thoughts from our own corrupt nature to Him who put on that nature in order to deliver it from corruption, and to fix our contemplations and our affections on Him who came to clothe us in His perfect righteousness, and through whom and in whom, if we are united to Him by a living faith, we too become righteous. . . . In the Christian view of man . . . the healthy normal state is not the subjective, but the objective, that in which, losing his own individual insulated life, he finds it again in Christ, that in which he does not make himself the object of his contemplation and action, but directs them both steadily and continually toward the will and the glory of God.[23]

Thomas Erskine, of Linlathen, used to take long drives on winter afternoons. He tells us that returning to his home with his face toward the east he

was attracted and interested by the frequent recurrence of the same natural phenomenon. The moon rose a little before the sun set, and had just the appearance of a thin bit of fleecy cloud, like a great many others, for in the hazy atmosphere its outline was not at all distinct. . . . At last it gradually distinguished itself from the rest by having always the same shape and the same place. . . . It was evidently a permanent thing amongst changeable things—an objective thing amongst subjective things.[24]

This proposed to his mind a spiritual counterpart. He felt that the clouds were like

exhalations from myself . . . suggestions of my own mind, continually liable to change through the modifications which they suffered from other thoughts; they were all decidedly subjective. . . . But I wanted and needed to have the consciousness of the actual presence of the great Objective in me,—not thoughts about Him, but Himself, or at least something which I was sure did not depend upon myself, but would always assert its own distinct independent reality, and which could not possibly be my own imagination, having this personal power and life in it, unmistakably.[25]

This most surely describes a healthy objectivity which transcends the fleeting impressionism of subjective experience, and rests the soul's hope on One who is outside and beyond our own feelings and states of mind, whose Word may be trusted even when our own "hearts condemn us" (I John 3:20). It is dangerous and demonic to make man the measure of all things. As Frederick W. Schroeder has said, "when man arrogates unto himself finality in matters of faith and morals, he is in effect exalting himself to the status of deity, thereby absolutizing the relative and relativizing the Absolute. This is human pride carried to . . . unprecedented heights."[26] The gosepl is the "good news" of what *God* has done, not of what has happened to us. It was here long before we experienced it, it is far broader than anything we can experience, and we limit it to our experience only at our peril.

In his sermon on the Canaanite woman in Matthew 15, Luther penetrated to the heart of the question of faith's lying beyond experience in the following words:

> This was written to comfort and teach us all to know how deeply God hides his grace for us and how we should cling, not to our feelings or thoughts about him, but strictly to his Word. . . . For this reason our heart must turn aside from such feelings and with firm faith in God's Word seize and cling to the Yes deep and hidden beneath and beyond the No, just as this woman, and give God his due when he judges us. Then we have won him and caught him in his own words.[27]

Turning now from the limitations of experience, let us try to see what relation our own experience of the gospel has to the realities which it embodies. We do have Christian experiences. As we indicated right at the start, God does His work *for* us, but then confronts us in such a way that He wants to do His work *in* us. His Word is "living and active, sharper than any two-edged sword" (Heb. 4:12). It is dynamic, it effects things. In the striking phrase of

Cromwell, God "spoke *things.*"[28] What is the relation of Christian experience to the thing experienced? How does our experience witness to that which has produced it? Professor Eduard Schweizer has raised this question in an interesting illustration. You have gone to the theater. I meet you a few days later and ask: "Tell me, what happened at the theater last Friday night?" You reply, "Oh, it was wonderful. I was deeply moved. Tears ran down my eyes. I was so excited that I could not sleep during the night. I have not been able to put it out of my mind since." I should have to say to you in return: "But you have not told me what happened at the theater. I did not ask what happened to your feelings, but what happened at the theater!"

Now unless the emotional experience here described was purely fictitious, or the result of a drug trip or some other hallucinative aberration, something really did happen at the theater. Unless the person involved is emotionally unstable, a highly charged experience of that sort must have had something solid behind it to produce it. In this sense, experience has some validity in that it points to something experienced. For normal people, experiences are not produced by nothing. As Scott Holland has put it,

> Experience always implies something more than our impression. If it were only an impression it would not be an experience. To be an experience it must be, in some measure, a fact. . . . If there was no element of reality, then we were mistaken in classing it as an experience. For experience is the coming together of ourselves with something else. . . . There is something in it which is "given"—something more than a subjective reaction.[29]

That is, if I should touch a bare electric wire which has no electric current in it and suddenly jump back and cry out in pain, that would not be a real experience. That would be a mere impression induced by the power of suggestion and the deceit of my senses. If, on the other hand, I touch a bare wire with current in it and then jump back and scream, it is a real experience. There is a reality there which meets me, something which is not the mere subjective power of suggestion, something which I cannot deny as real. I experience it, but experience testifies to the reality of the thing experienced. The reality without which the experience could not be is the electricity. I can have the experience only if it is there.

So it is with the Christian faith. It is a matter of experience, but the thing experienced is the center of it all. And if there is nothing there to experience, the whole affair of faith would have no value for us. Our need is to experience the faith, but to lift it out of the psychological realm which makes it an affair of my states of mind, or of positive thinking, or of a device to get something out of it, and turns my attention to the reality lying beyond the experience. In other words, in all genuine Christian experience, the focus is more on the God who produces the experience than on the one who experiences Him. Hence, although we must have a genuine experience of God in Christ, although we must become "new creatures" of His love, although "old things" must pass away for us and all things "become new," yet the wonder of it all is the God who creates the new creation. His glory in the new creation is paramount. My experience is the sphere within which this functions, but it is not its source. My subjectivity is under the authority of the objective God. This authority, as Forsyth remarked, "is indeed *within* experience, but it is not the authority *of* experience, it is an authority *for* experience, it is an authority experienced."[30] What we need, then, is not the authority of experience, but the experience of authority. We need to find outside ourselves that which so commands us that we have no alternative but to bow before it with a glad acquiescence. This is to experience authority. As Harris E. Kirk once said: "Authority is like fire; it is not something to be argued with; you must come to terms with it. It carries its own evidence . . . the authenticity of an experience that cannot be questioned."[31]

In the realm of the Christian faith, we are limited to the testimony of others about the Christian facts. We have not had direct experience of Jesus. We did not live with Him. We did not hear Him teach. We did not watch Him die. We did not meet with Him when raised. We were not present at the Ascension. We did not participate in Pentecost, when His Spirit returned to dwell in the life of the church. We are among those "that have not seen, and yet have believed" (John 20:29). The big question for us, then, is whether there was reality behind the experience recorded in the New Testament. Was the apostolic experience self-induced? Can it be accounted for on mere psychological and subjective grounds as mere impression? Or was the apostolic experience a response to a "given," a reaction to a genuine current in the wire, a witness to that which happened *for* them before it happened *in* them, a sure evidence that they were in touch with the "God from whom all blessings flow"? In other words, in reading the New Testament record, are we experiencing the authority of the real, or wallowing in the morass of an emotional binge produced by no objective creative act? If nothing lay behind it, we should then have to account for the creation of the Christian church out of nothing, and for its long and glorious history (in spite of its dark spots). How could this be done? To account for the New Testament message on any grounds other than those on which it accounts for itself would seem to suggest an effect greater than its cause, or an effect without a cause, and to incur the scorn of Thomas Carlyle: "O men, great is your infidel-faith!"[32]

Scott Holland sums it up well, when he says: ". . . If, therefore, [the apostolic record] commend itself to us and take possession of our hearts and minds," it is because

> what is felt to be given in them, to be pressing through them, to be transmitted by them, is the compelling force of an

historical fact. . . . Their utmost effort is but to interpret what it was that happened. It was done before their eyes. It took hold of their being. It ratified its reality by every faculty that they possessed. It was Jesus Christ, dead on the Cross, risen from the grave, alive and reigning. . . . If it did not happen, then their faith is vain. No value remains in impression or idea, in thought, or imagination, or feeling. . . . If it happened, it happened: and happened like that. So we are persuaded by those who came under its dominance.[33]

Their experience, then, not ours, is normative and authoritative over us. Let us utilize their witness to bring us into touch with the living Lord to whom they bore witness in such fashion that we shall share their conviction and know in our own experience the power which changed their lives and the joys of which they spoke. But let us focus our gaze through their testimony on the Christ who produced their experience and ours, not trusting our experiences but trusting Him. And let us point men not to ourselves and our experience, but to Him.

A traveler in Tennessee, coming round a curve in a narrow road, met a farmer on foot. He stopped, and asked: "How far is it to the Smoky Mountains." Said the farmer: "One mile, and a look!" How far is it to the experience of authority for us? The Scriptures, and a look to Him who said: "Look unto me, and be ye saved, all the ends of the earth: for I am God, and there is none else" (Isa. 45:22, KJV).

Chapter Five

The Biblical Basis
of the Authority of the Church

This chapter leads us into difficult terrain. Its subject has polarized the church in our time. There are wide differences of opinion over it among very good people. It has divided friends, it has alienated members of families, it has produced tensions in church courts, it has set up conflict between the church and the world. One would prefer to bypass this question if for no other reason than he hates to add to the discord already present. Furthermore, in a matter of such profound consequence, one can only render his own reasoned opinion in the consciousness that he does not have final wisdom about it and that his bungling efforts might serve to worsen the cause rather than better it. Unfortunately, however, it is a question that we cannot bypass, for it will not let us alone. It not only obtrudes itself into our consciousness, but forces its way into our decisions.

Regrettably, too, this is a subject about which almost anything that one says will likely be misunderstood. On questions that involve us practically and emotionally at such a deep level, it is difficult for us to hear what is said. We tend to read into statements meanings which are not intended but which seem to bolster our own preconceived views or our wishes. This subject, therefore, creates strange bedfellows. One finds himself in accord at certain specific points with others who welcome his comradeship, but from whose basic presuppositions or broad outlook he would recoil. This is a day of extremism. On this subject, therefore, as at so many points, if one does not wholly align himself with either party to an issue, he is theologically lonely, caught in a no-man's-land of theological battle where he is shot at from both sides. We take up the subject, therefore, with a good deal of fear and trembling, confessing that we are not as sure of our ground at this point as we have been at others, yet hoping that our discussion will at least produce some thought and not be further polarizing, nor totally fruitless.

I should like to begin by proposing that whatever our views of the involvement the church should have in society, the church has a unique task, which if it neglects will simply not be done. That task is theological. If, therefore, the church should get so wrapped up in causes and claims that she neglects her unique function in society, she is recreant to her duty and in the long run will not only destroy herself but be a liability rather than an asset to society. If the function of the church is only to make society better, then I can agree with her critics that in her present form she is a drag on society and is wasting resources which could be better used. Direct social action can be undertaken much more effectively by those trained in sociology, economics, political science, and the strategies of invading power structures and organizing groups for social change. Departments of universities already exist for this purpose. For the church, therefore, to spend millions on theological seminaries and church buildings and programs of Christian education and the cultivation of congregational conclaves, is a social waste, and the sooner that it comes to an end the better. If, however, the church has a unique task that cannot be done by social and economic and political maneuvering, and cannot be carried forward by any other group of men, then its expenditures to maintain its own life in the world may well be justified. If there is a theological task to be done without which the world cannot live, which may be even more important than the social, economic, and political tasks, then, despite all criticism the church cannot surrender this task without failing both humanity and her Lord.

What is the church's unique task? It is the theological task of relating men rightly to God. Social amelioration is the fruit, not the root, of faith. The first commandment is this: "You shall love the Lord your God with all your heart, and with all your soul, and with all your mind" (Matt. 22:37). Then, the second commandment follows: "You shall love your neighbor as yourself" (vs. 39). The church is involved in both tasks, but its priorities must be regulated by the priority laid down in the Bible—first, the love of God—"This is the great and first commandment"—and second, the love of men.

I am fully aware of recent attempts to reverse these priorities. It is argued that the priority is one of importance rather than of sequence, of degree or rank rather than of time. The love of God is first in the sense that it is of ultimate concern, but it is an outgrowth of the love of one's neighbor and is therefore secondary in sequence. This would seem to be an unnatural twist to these words, a theological *tour de forcé*. Although Scripture elsewhere suggests that failing to love one's neighbor indicates that one does not love God (I John 2:9; 4:20), this by no means suggests that love of God is dependent upon, or an outgrowth from, love of neighbor. Theologically, and I believe psychologically as well—for why should I care a whit about my brother apart from the fact that he is a man for whom Christ died, and therefore a mutual object of that love of God which has first laid hold of me before I can see my brother as one loved of God?—the natural sequence of these words gives a *time* priority to the first commandment. This is affirmed by Eduard Schweizer, in his recent commentary on Mark: "When Mark introduces [love of neighbor] expressly as a second commandment, he does so in order to indicate the proper sequence.

Though love for God is something concrete and can be experienced only as one exercises love for his neighbor, still everything depends upon the recognition that the latter becomes possible only on the basis of the former."[1]

The church is not separate from culture, but it is rooted elsewhere than in culture. The church is *"in* the world" but not *"of* the world" (John 17:11, 14). Its sources are deep in the unseen and the eternal, its trust is in "something more than civilization, and something outside history."[2] Furthermore, it is to go *"into* the world" (John 17:18), but it is to take to the world more than mere human service. It is "evangelical service" which the church takes to the world. It brings a gospel of divine redemption rather than of human amelioration. It insists that our sin is not first against our brother, but against God. It brings the light of the invisible world into the world of the visible and reminds men that if they should gain the whole world but lose their own life—life which is fellowship with God—they have no profit. As James Denney put it: "The Church does nothing unless it does the deepest things; it does nothing unless it prevails on sinful men to have peace with God through our Lord Jesus Christ, and to walk in love even as He loved us. Let us fix our minds on this as the first and supreme interest, and everything else will come out in its proper place."[3] We must keep before men the fact, which perhaps most of our generation do not know, that

> *yonder all before us lie*
> *Deserts of vast eternity.*[4]

We must remind them, in the words of John Baillie, "that our earthly existence [is] not primarily of value for its own sake, but only as the forecourt of a greater glory yet to be."[5] Worthy though the things of time be, we must press "the greater claim of the interests of eternity."[6] We must claim men as citizens of eternity, so that they give only "qualified hope" to human ideals in history, and that they give it in a fashion that would, even if that hope "were to suffer complete shipwreck, leave [their] ultimate hope as securely anchored as before."[7]

So, as Forsyth said, ". . . The Churches can do nothing permanent and nothing final for human welfare till the soul gets its own. The Church is not 'first of all a working Church.' . . . [It is not conducting a 'kingdom-of-God industry.'] It is there to feed the soul with eternal reality, to establish, strengthen, and settle the soul upon the Rock of Ages."[8] The value of the church is not determined by its "cultural benefits," by its practical effectiveness in securing human amelioration, but in its effectiveness in confronting men with a holy God, in relation to whom our sin against our fellowman fades into insignificance. In fact, we shall never really know our sin against our fellowman until we make the outcry of the Psalmist: "Against thee, and thee only, have I sinned, and done this evil in thy sight" (Ps. 51:4). We know sins, but do we know sin? We revolt from specific manifestations of evil, but do we revolt from evil itself in the light of our total guilt before God? The questions are dramatized in some of the protests today. The sin of war is protested, but what about the sin which produces war? And what about the sins of drugs and of sex and of pride and of belligerence and of self-righteousness and of dominating the wills of others? We shall never deal effectively with our *sins,* until we deal with the deeper problem of our *sin.* And we shall never deal with this deeper problem of our sin until we recover a sense of the absolute holiness of God, and see not only certain manifestations of wrong, but our own guilt, in the depths of our very natures, in the light of that holiness on the cross.

But is this central and unique function of the church being discharged today, or have we gotten sidetracked? Are we under the indictment of Forsyth when he said we are

> producing reform . . . faster than we are producing faith. . . .
> We are putting all our religious capital into the extension of

our business, and carrying nothing to reserve or insurance. We are mortgaging and starving the future. We are not seeking first the Kingdom of God and His holiness. . . . We are merely running the kingdom; and we are running it without the cross—with the cross perhaps on our sign, but not in our centre. We have the old trade mark, but what does that matter in a dry and thirsty land where no water is, if the artesian well on our premises is going dry? . . . The attention of the Christian public . . . has been deflected towards social sympathies, at the cost of personal, experimental, and I will say ethical religion. . . . For we have lost the sense of sin, which is the central issue of all ethic because it turns on the relation of the conscience to the conscience of God. . . . Religious sympathies or energies are not Christian faith.[9]

One often today hears the charge that there is as much, if not more, Christianity outside the church than within it. Forsyth adds:

It would be true enough if Christianity meant decent living, nice ways, precious kindness, business honour, ardent philanthropy, and public righteousness. But all these fine and worthy things are quite compatible with the absence of personal communion with God, personal faith as Christ claims it, in the sense of personal experience of God in Jesus Christ, personal repentance, and personal peace in Christ as our eternal life.[10]

Is the church producing this personal awareness of the living Christ in men's lives today? If not, are we fulfilling our distinctive role in the world, whatever else we are doing? Perhaps Christ's word to us is, "these you ought to have done, without neglecting the others" (Matt. 23:23).

About two generations ago, Dr. R. W. Dale, of Carr's Lane Chapel in Birmingham, England, took a very active part in political matters for many years as a Christian clergyman. In his maturer years, he began to question the wisdom of this. In a letter to a friend he wrote: ". . . As the shadows lengthen I am more disposed than in past years to think that perhaps my 'vocation' . . . requires an abstention from the actual conflict of political life."[11] He reread some articles he had written in his early ministry, in which he "deprecated the waste of strength occasioned by intermeddling with politics and other matters lying outside the direct line" of the work of the church. He concluded that "it seemed odd that at the beginning of my ministry I should have seen—apparently with such clearness—the truth which has come home to me . . . at the close of it. It is a clear case of seeing the better path and choosing the worse. Alas!"[12]

When the Congregational Union, the official fellowship of all the Congregational Churches, began to take direct action with regard to political matters, Dale withdrew from it. He did not believe that "the Congregational Union should be regarded as a court of review which is under obligation to discuss at its annual assemblies the morality of all the political events of the year."[13] When he was accused of severing religion from politics, he replied: "I can sever religion from no political question; it does not follow that every political question is the proper concern of the Union. There are many grave things into which religion enters with which the Union has nothing to do."[14] He most certainly did not think that the church should not influence political decisions, but, says A. W. W. Dale, he came

> to the parting of the ways in the choice of methods by which the Christian Church should attempt to regenerate the social life of nations. For himself he was convinced that the Church was in its very essence a religious institution established for religious ends; that social and political reforms, however desirable, were not the objects of its activity; and that so to regard them would be to degrade the Church into a political organization. The dominion of the State over the Church he regarded as perilous to religion; the dominion of the Church over the State as perilous to both.[15]

He said: "I have the gravest fears of what will come from the present passion of some excellent persons to capture Christian churches and to change them into political and municipal caucuses. . . . I have no objection to political caucuses; they are necessary; but God forbid that any church of which I may ever be minister or member should be a caucus."[16]

The great statesman Edmund Burke offered a similar opinion near the end of the eighteenth century. In his *Reflections on the Revolution in France,* he referred to a sermon by an eminent nonconforming minister,

> in which there are some good moral and religious sentiments, and not ill expressed, mixed up in a sort of porridge of various political opinions and reflections. . . . I looked on that sermon as the public declamation of a man much connected with caballers, and intriguing philosophers; with political theologians, and theological politicians, . . . yet politics and the pulpit are terms that have little agreement. No sound ought to be heard in the church but the healing voice of Christian charity. The cause of civil liberty and civil government gains as little as that of religion by this confusion of duties. Those who quit their proper character, to assume what does not belong to them, are, for the greater part, ignorant both of the character they leave, and of the character they assume. Wholly unacquainted with the world in which they are so fond of meddling, and inexperienced in all of its affairs, on which they pronounce with so much confidence, they have nothing of politics but the passions they excite. Surely the church is a place where one day's truce ought to be allowed to the dissensions and animosities of mankind.[17]

This last statement would be questioned by many; but even if a "truce" may not be desirable in the church, the church does not remain the church unless "the dissensions and animosities of mankind" are seen in a different light there than outside the church, and unless they are dealt with in "the healing voice of Christian charity."

Have the fears of Forsyth, Dale, and Burke that the church by becoming deeply and directly involved in political and social issues would lose her unique mission been justified in our time? Each one must decide for himself. It at least cannot be said that any one of these men had these fears because he was trying to escape individual responsibility. All had a deep involvement in the social and political problems of their time. In the light of present developments in the life of the church, it might be well at least to ponder their judgment in making our own.

It hardly needs documenting that many of the church's own adherents are seeing "relevance" in the church only to the extent that it becomes a direct instrument in solving the problems of poverty, race, war, ignorance, and prejudice. One would assume that no one worthy of the name Christian would be indifferent to these grave social, economic, and political questions. But is the church's concern with these issues to be of no deeper quality than that of other "action" groups? And if these problems fail of solution, does the church have no word of hope for that situation of failure? Is there not a "freedom which transcends all social situations and may express itself even within and under tyranny"?[18]

The time will come, says Jesus, when the structures of human existence utterly collapse, when nations are distressed and perplexed, and men's hearts are faint "with fear and with foreboding of what is coming on the world. . . . Now when these things begin to take place," He counsels, "look up and raise your heads, because your redemption is drawing near" (Luke 21:25-28). One does not have to be able fully to clarify what these strange words mean to see in them the declaration of a liberation which transcends many of the current hopes for human justice, a liberation which it is the church's unique task to proclaim along with other forms of human liberation. It was this liberation that enabled the Jubilee Assembly of the Evangelical Church of the Czech Brethren to proclaim, even after the terrible events of the Russian invasion of August 21, 1968, that Christ's "work of reconciliation . . . brings hope in the face of death and nothingness."[19]

On the other hand, if our hopes for human justice are

wholly fulfilled, would the work of the church then be done? Suppose poverty, racism, war, ignorance, and prejudice were no more, would the word of the gospel no longer be needed? On his last visit to this country, the late Dr. Josef Hromadka, a Czech theologian who taught for some time in the United States, said that at least some of the Communist thinkers in Czechoslovakia were saying in effect: "We have had our revolution, we have eliminated class distinctions, we have overcome the drag of the evils of capitalism, but we have not yet arrived. What lack we yet?" And they had asked him to lecture to them at the University of Prague on prayer! Maybe, after all, what Professor Hromadka had told them twenty-five years earlier was true, that there are depths in human nature to which the gospel speaks that lie deeper than those needs represented by the social, political, and economic revolutionary movements of our day.

And while advocates of "revolutionary theology" do battle with the forces of evil entrenched in the social order, can the church abdicate its responsibility of reminding them that all power tends toward corruption, and that unless we offer men inner freedom from thralldom to the powers of darkness through the liberating work of Jesus Christ, the exorcising of the demons they seek to cast out could open the way for more demons to enter, leaving the last state worse than the first? To take power from some so that others may have it, but to leave those others outside the sphere of Christ's mastery of the demonic, is a reshuffling that may exchange the personnel of ruler and ruled but will only perpetuate a corrupt situation in other hands. The issue is not so much who rules and who is ruled, but whether the ruler rules selfishly or responsibly and whether those ruled accept authority or rebel against it selfishly. There is a moving and pathetic, but very profound, passage in the recent play *The Man in the Glass Box,* based on the trial of Adolf Eichmann. At the end of an eight-minute oration in praise of his Fuehrer and his power to lay hold of men with his eloquence and promises, the man in the glass box shouts: "People of Israel, had he chosen you, you, too, would have followed!" This is no anti-Semitic indictment of Israel, but a profound analysis of the dark depths in all human nature. After all, Hitler set out to right wrongs, to establish justice for those whom he believed had been oppressed, to "put down the mighty from their thrones" in order to exalt "those of low degree." But he illustrated that of which Paul Minear reminds us when he says that the "heavens" of the "architects of utopias" are

> constructed out of forlorn desires, desires that the world has created and then frustrated. Crusaders . . . increase the disorder by trying to force their dreams upon their fellows. . . . Thus the world creates hopelessness that is greatest in the hearts of those who hope for the utopias that the world, by its negative logic, encourages. . . . When the world locates truly the enemies of its real peace, then it will find use for this archaic armor: "the shield of faith, . . . the sword of the Spirit, which is the word of God" (Eph. 6:16).[20]

Minear's warning is seconded by Brevard Childs:

> The threat of a new American theological liberalism that finds its warrant for social action in a vague reference to "making human the structures of society" has already made strong inroads into the life of the church. . . . The majority of the clichés that one associates with radical theology have roots within the Biblical tradition: a "prophetic" ministry against the religious establishment, social justice for all men, the idolatry of nationalism, the freedom to live and love boldly in the present moment, radical secularity as the grounds for recovering one's full humanity, the search for authenticity, the humanizing of society, etc. It is of great importance that these concepts be filled with a content that is informed by the study of the Bible. Nothing would be more unfortunate for theology [than] if these concepts were distorted and misunderstood in order to serve a totally alien function from their original intent.[21]

Unless this warning is heeded, the church's authority may be totally transformed from the authority of a self-authenticating Word of God heard from beyond herself in the disclosure of the divine nature through the redemptive work of Jesus Christ into a mere humanitarian response of human sympathy. Then the

> formula "Hear the word of God" is only an idiom for saying: "This is what I as a sensitive religious person think." The effect is that the analogy of a "prophetic ministry" is maintained by reducing the prophets in size. Rather than the Biblical tradition serving as a norm, the reverse is true. Modern human experience becomes the norm for what is of value in the tradition.[22]

Many modern attempts at social reorganization bear witness to the fact that even "atheism is not incompatible with a great experiment in social reconstruction" and that the "finest humanitarianism may prevail while yet the man who exemplifies it feels himself to be an orphan in the world."[23] The unique task of the Christian church is to call to men, "Behold, your God!" and then to summon them to turn toward their brother. It is only in His light that we shall catch a true perspective on the deepest needs of the human heart. Without this, we shall tend to "dress [the] people's wound, but skin-deep only" (Jer. 6:14, NEB).

The second thing that I believe should concern us today is the danger the church faces of being taken over by groups whose ethos and motivation are alien to the Christian faith. There are certain goals which the church may share with other groups and toward which their combined energies may be wisely directed. But the motivation behind the church's action is totally different from that of other groups. The church needs to keep this in mind and maintain her autonomy in relation to these groups whose dynamic comes from another source. Dr. Hromadka illustrated this pointedly some years ago. Against the advice of many of his friends, he left the United States to return to his native Czechoslovakia after the Communist take-over there. He wanted to try to serve the Czech Church and to work out a way of Christian living under Communist dominance. He once was asked to speak to a great throng in the public square in Prague. His speech followed several Communist addresses, and he told the crowd boldly, "I share many of the social goals of these, my friends; but I do so for a very different reason. I share these goals because I believe in the resurrection of Jesus Christ!" [24] This is brave and clear Christian witness! It keeps the church autonomous, although it stands beside others in ministry. It seems rather easy for the church to maintain her autonomy in a Communist land, for Communists are by definition atheists and therefore cannot openly work through the church. It was different in Hitler's Germany. There the Nazis infiltrated the church and took it over, save for the Confessing Church, which resisted. Many people could not understand why Karl Barth took such a strong stand against the Nazis and did not against the Communists. The reason lies right here. He said that the church could survive in Communist lands, for they knew who their enemy was. The lines were clearly drawn. However much the two groups might work together, the sources of their life were understood to be alien from each other. The Nazis, however, tried to turn the church into an agent of their designs. They Germanized the church, modified its teaching, sought to change the sources of its spiritual authority. The church was in danger of her life by being taken over by forces alien to her own genius.

There was historical precedent for this. The religious outlook of the second-century Gnostics paralleled Christianity at some points, but properly understood was altogether alien to it. The Gnostics found the church a ready-made platform for their ideas and an already existing organization for their propaganda, if they could take it over. The danger lay in the fact that at a superficial level the aims of Gnosticism and of the church were the same. Gnosticism was longing for redemption, for example, and so was the church—but salvation for Gnosticism "was a romantic-idealistic not a moral-historic salvation; it sought deliverance from estrangement in the world and from the material aspect of existence [how much like those movements today which are trying to overcome alienation and free themselves from our materialistic values!], not deliverance from a guilty estrangement from God into communion with him."[25] The church, therefore, had to resist being taken over by it.

There are movements today which see the church as a ready-made organization that can be used to advance their own ends, movements which, if they could gain total control of the world, would immediately eliminate the church as one of their first acts. To all such the church must insist that, as Forsyth said, "God is not the world's greatest asset but its eternal Lord."[26] We must not permit others to dupe us into a shallow conception of the kingdom of God which "does not realize its essential otherworldliness [however this-worldly its manifestations], its vastness so great that its consummation can only be beyond earthly history."[27] To help such people in the long run, the church may have to resist them temporarily, maintaining her own autonomy to do her own distinctive work in confronting men with Him who is "the source of eternal salvation to all who obey him" (Heb. 5:9). She may, at this point, have to follow her Lord who "always stood for God against the men he would save."[28]

A third consideration is this: It is possible that if the church stuck to her unique task of bringing men into the sphere of God's redemption in Christ she might be more productive in effecting social change than she now is with direct methods. It is, of course, not true that one can make a better society merely by making better men. There are corporate manifestations of evil over which individual men have no power. These must be dealt with. But it is true that one cannot make a better society without making better men! And the need for better men is the greatest need of the world today. We bewail corruption and bribery and cheating and sidestepping in business and government. But these are not impersonal. It is only *men* who are corrupt, who give and take bribes, who cheat, and sidestep. If these things are to be overcome, we need more than laws, good and necessary though they be. It can be done only by producing men who are incorruptible. I recently heard Ann Landers, of newspaper column fame, speak at a Rotary Club Ladies Day in Pittsburgh. She sees a pretty good cross-section of American life through receiving nearly 400,000 letters a year. Somebody asked her in a question period, what was the one most vivid impression she received from all these letters. After a moment of thought, she said that it was the impression of the breakdown of personal integrity in American life. If *men* do not have integrity, laws will not achieve it. If, then, the church were doing her work of producing men of integrity, if it were known that a man who professes the name of Christ was impervious to bribery and above corruption, what do you suppose might happen in society?

In our efforts to produce social betterment, have we really taken the measure of our enemy? Do we know what we are up against? Human beings are natively self-centered. And how do you get men to change at the very core of their lives? How do you get men to surrender their self-centeredness? That is the profoundest problem known to man. The only way to do it is to replace the self with God. And that is exactly what Jesus Christ proposes to do with men! If, then, the church were working harder at this task, is it possible that we would influence the world far more than we are now doing with our efforts at direct intervention? James Denney thought so: " . . . The Church which cultivates in all its members the spirit of humanity, the spirit of liberty, justice, generosity, and mercy, will do more for the coming of God's kingdom than if it plunged into the thick of every conflict, or offered its mediation in every dispute."[28a] This was seconded by Forsyth, who said: "We can never fully say 'My brother!' till we have heartily said, 'My God'; and we can never heartily say 'My God' till we have humbly said 'My Guilt.' "[29] "You must always tell men that they can never be right with each other except as they are right with God in Christ and in the atoning Cross of Christ."[30]

Dr. Dale once pondered the problem of the sudden demise of Puritan influence in England:

> ... There is something startling in the sudden extinction of the fires which burnt during the Commonwealth; twenty years after Cromwell's death the fervour and zeal were almost gone; twenty years later still they had quite vanished. The question assailed me, whether the explanation did not lie in part in the premature attempt to apply to the political order the laws of a diviner kingdom and to do it by direct political action.[31]
>
> There have been two methods in which the Christian Church has exerted its power over the ethical life of the kingdoms in which it has existed, and over the political action of those kingdoms. For three centuries it was content to address itself immediately to the great work of drawing those within its reach to the acceptance of the Lord Jesus Christ as the Lord and Redeemer of men. It disciplined their character; it breathed into them a new spirit; they reached higher and nobler ethical principles, and large changes were wrought upon society as the result of that work. Then came a time when the Church was impatient of the slow progress which it made by that method; and if we descend a few centuries later we shall find the great Church of Western Christendom directly interfering as a church in the social and political affairs of nations. ... But we have come to the conclusion that the interference of organized churches with organized political societies has proved after all a false method of effecting the great objects of the Christian gospel. ... I have always felt that the line to be taken is this: that the churches should do all they can in the power of the grace and truth of Christ to renew and sanctify all whom they reach; and that then Christian men—as

citizens, not as members of churches—should appear in the community to discharge their duties to it, under the control of the spirit and law of Christ. The Papacy dealt with imperial power. There seems now to have come a great chance to the Free Churches of the country to deal with democratic power.... I believe that we shall not hasten the triumph of the principles for which we care—shall not hasten the securing of the ends on which our hearts are set—by any such organised interference of church with municipal and political life.[32]

The very opposite of the diminishing influence of Puritanism in seventeenth-century England is to be seen in the eighteenth-century England of John Wesley. John Alfred Faulkner, one of Wesley's interpreters, says of him:

I do not find that Wesley brought forward any new views of society or of political economy, ... He took the world as he found it, he worked with such laws and institutions as were in vogue; he did not disown the right of private property, the right of accumulation, the right of monarchy, the right of Parliament to tax.... On all such questions he stood for the *status quo*. His work was not to change laws or institutions, but to change men.[33]

. . . .

He had no social program, except the Pauline one of humble obedience to the powers that be. He was not a reformer, not an agitator. He did little more than reecho the words which once sounded down the Jordan valley: "Repent, for the kingdom of heaven is at hand." ... His great work was to make men the sons of God in truth.[34]

How did he come out in his efforts? What was his influence? Faulkner answers: "It brought it about—or at least it was one of the chief factors in bringing it about—that social, economic, and political reform in England was to go forward in peaceable channels, not by way of cataclysm, as in France then and in Russia now, but by way of quiet but inevitable evolution."[35] Lest the reader dismiss this as merely a prejudiced judgment by a religiously sympathetic writer, let me quote a remarkable passage from the English historian William Lecky, who could hardly be accused of being partial toward Wesley.

He wrote (and as you read this remarkable quotation, ask yourself if you have heard any more vivid description of what is going on in America today):

> Great as was the importance of the evangelical revival [sparked by Wesley] in stimulating these [philanthropic] efforts, it had other consequences of perhaps wider and more enduring influence. Before the close of the century in which it appeared, a spirit had begun to circulate in Europe threatening the very foundations of society and of belief. The revolt against the supernatural theory of Christianity which had been conducted by Voltaire and the encyclopaedists; the material conception of man and of the universe, which sprang from the increased study of physical science and from the metaphysics of Condillac and Helvetius; the wild social dreams which Rousseau had clothed in such transcendent eloquence; the misery of a high-spirited people ground to the dust by unnecessary wars and by partial and unjust taxation; the imbecility and corruption of rulers and priests, had together produced in France a revolutionary spirit which in its intensity and in its proselytizing fervor was unequaled since the days of the Reformation. It was soon felt in many lands. Millions of fierce and ardent natures were intoxicated by dreams of an impossible equality and complete social and political reorganization. Many old abuses perished, but a tone of thought and feeling was introduced into European life which could only lead to anarchy and at length to despotism, and was beyond all others fatal to that measured and ordered freedom which can alone endure. Its chief characteristics were a hatred of all constituted authority, an insatiable appetite for change, a habit of regarding rebellion as the normal as well as the noblest form of political self-sacrifice, a disdain for all compromise, a contempt for all tradition, a desire to level all ranks and subvert all establishments, a determination to seek progress, not by the slow and cautious amelioration of existing institutions, but by sudden, violent, revolutionary changes. Religion, property, civil authority, and domestic life were all assailed, and doctrines incompatible with the very existence of government were embraced

by multitudes with the fervor of a religion. England on the whole escaped the contagion. Many causes conspired to save her, but among them the prominent place must, I believe, be given to the new and vehement religious enthusiasm which was at the very time passing through the middle and lower classes of the people, which had enlisted in the service a large proportion of the wilder and more impetuous reformers, and which recoiled with horror from the anti-Christian tenets that were associated with the Revolution in France.[36]

I think it is safe to say that, since St. Paul, there has been no one single ministry that was more productive of social change than that of John Wesley. Yet he did not set out to effect social change. His recorded sermons are almost without exception solid gospel sermons, with little or no direct social application, save as the virtues of redeemed lives affect society. He changed *men,* through the power of the Holy Spirit, and they changed institutions and society.

At the risk of too great frequency, let me refer once more to Dr. Dale, whose forty-year ministry was inseparably associated with the city of Birmingham, England. He says:

I look back upon the history of this town. Some twenty years ago, I remember, there was a great and successful movement for reforming our administration and ennobling it. The men that took part in that movement had learnt the principles on which they acted, and caught the spirit by which they were inspired, very largely in the Nonconformist churches of Birmingham. . . . I do not believe that if the Nonconformist churches of Birmingham had been organised to secure the results which were achieved by that municipal reform, their organised efforts would have been half as effective as the efforts of their individual members as citizens in the community.[37]

Maybe the twentieth century so differs from the seventeenth, eighteenth, and nineteenth centuries that a similar methodology now would not obtain a like result. On the other hand, this examination of the methods by which the church sought to influence society in those days could well be instructive for us. Perhaps we could be more effective in achieving social results if we regained confidence in our own theological and redemptive task and stuck to our own task, rather than merely joining others in an effort to be direct agents of social change.

An outstanding instance of one who felt that preaching the gospel was more important than dealing with immediate political and social themes is Dr. William Hoge, brother of the famous Moses D. Hoge. He had been called not long before the Civil War to be one of the pastors of the Brick Presbyterian Church in New York City. He was much beloved, and extremely influential in his preaching. Within less than six months of his arrival extra chairs had regularly to be placed in the aisles to accommodate the crowds. Then the war came. In a frenzied time, when emotions were high and church courts were making political pronouncements (from which the Presbyterian Church has not fully recovered after a hundred years!), how easy it would have been for Dr. Hoge to have taken the cause of the South into the pulpit. His brother's biographer tells us, however, that although

> his heart was with his own people in the South . . . the vows of God were upon him, and as long as his people would receive the gospel at his lips, no political or personal consideration could be allowed to break the bond. The things of the kingdom must be first. The pulpits of the city were ringing with politics; he preached the gospel. Crowds greater than before hung on his ministry, for there were thousands in that great city who were asking for bread and receiving stones. If it was his mission to feed them he would stay at any cost; though friends in the South were already murmuring.[38]

One Sunday morning, Dr. Hoge's colleague preached a politically partisan sermon. An expectant crowd gathered at the vesper service, expecting Dr. Hoge to answer him. The hymn before the sermon was William Cowper's hymn,

"There is a fountain filled with blood." Dr. Hoge read it before the singing. When he reached the last stanza, he closed the book, took a step back from the pulpit, and quoted from memory:

> *Ere since by faith I saw the stream*
> *Thy flowing wounds supply,*
> *Redeeming love has been my theme,*
> *And shall be till I die.*

The crowd then knew that they would get no politics in that sermon.

Who was right? The morning preacher, or Dr. Hoge? Only eternity will tell. But from this perspective, one can join with many others who at that time deplored "the madness of the times in which it was possible that 'a faithful minister of the gospel may be proscribed for his private, unobtruded political views.' "[39] Some weeks later, when Dr. Hoge was finally forced from his pulpit, he devoted his farewell sermon to a "testimony against the preaching of anything but the religion of Christ from a Christian pulpit."[40] He insisted that as a private citizen he had studied the questions of the day and formed his private judgment. He insisted, too, that as a citizen he had the right to express these opinions. But, he insisted, "he had not forgotten, meantime, that he was also a minister of the gospel, and that therefore it became him to utter his opinions unobtrusively, 'giving no offense in anything that the ministry be not blamed.' "[41]

He had prayed for the President of the United States *and* for the authorities of the Confederate States. He had prayed for the welfare of the soldiers on both sides of the conflict. He said that his sermons had "simply been, as far as I had strength to make them, scriptural, gospel sermons."[42] He referred to a published sermon of his on "Blind Bartimaeus," in which there was the following language:

They have let him (Bartimaeus) know that the Healer of the blind is near; and I am sure that nothing they could say about anything else could make up for not telling him that. The most eloquent harangue on the politics of the times, though Pilate and Herod and Caesar, and Roman eagles, and Jewish banners and liberty, and nationality and destiny, had rolled with splendid imagery through sounding periods, would have been a sad exchange for those simple words, "Jesus of Nazareth passeth by." Nor would Aristotle's keenest logic, nor Plato's finest speculation, have served a whit better. The man was blind, and wanted his eyes opened; and till this was done, these things, however set forth, were but trash and mockery.[43]

And what reward did Dr. Hoge get for this approach? He got his house burned to the ground, with all its contents, his family escaping only with their lives. But even after that, in his farewell sermon, he maintained the same mood as before, saying: "I fear we are just beginning to reap the bitter fruits which political preaching and political action in our ecclesiastical courts are to bring forth. . . . May God raise mightier voices than mine everywhere to sound the alarm before all our churches are made fearful and scandalous spectacles of strife and confusion, and God's blessed Spirit is grieved utterly away!"[44] It is plain how costly to his inner life it was to hold to this conviction. He continued:

. . . Ever since the beginning of this national conflict, my heart has yearned towards my beloved South, and especially the dear Commonwealth of Virginia. I have longed to share their privations, their dangers, and their destiny, whether of humiliation or triumph; but all these feelings I was ready to sacrifice on the altar of Christ and His cause. And I did sacrifice them. God gave me the joyous capacity to absorb myself in my work as a Christian minister. Having abundantly declared, by my conduct and in this discourse, that I place this sacred relation of pastor and people above every national question, I could never have severed it for such a cause as this, weighty though I feel it to be in itself.[45]

There will be difference of opinion in appraising such a course as he took. But I for one would stake a firm guess that when we stand before the final judgment seat of Christ Dr. Hoge will stand not one whit below the "political" preachers of that turbulent period, and he may even stand somewhat taller. When He who is the final Judge, who once replied when He was asked to pronounce an economic judgment between brothers, "Who made me a . . . divider over you?" (Luke 12:14), sifts the chaff from the wheat, it may well be that such as Dr. Hoge will fare as well as or better than those who insist that their pulpits are given them to urge certain specific courses of social or political action. Only God can know. The rest of us will have to cast our lot where conscience demands. But is it at least not worth pondering whether the spirit manifested by Dr. Hoge might create a church more productive of redemptive social and political action than the present methods of many?

One final consideration—although the subject is not thereby exhausted. We have argued in earlier chapters that God's authority over us at its highest and best is spiritual authority—that self-authenticating authority which vindicates itself through His self-revelation in His Son and functions in our lives not by coercion and raw might but by our glad acceptance of it and obedient response to it. This is the authority of Christ. The church bears no authority save the authority of Christ. There is not space here to deal with the subject in its broad dimensions, but it is plain that in the New Testament Christ delegated at least some of His authority to the church. The point with which I would like to conclude is this: If the church bears the authority of Christ, and if that authority is purely spiritual and persuasive, is not the church at her best in the exercise of authority when she is persuasive and convincing rather than coercive? Are we not tempted to forget that it is "not by might, nor by power, but by [God's] Spirit" (Zech.

4:6) that the work of the church is to go forward in the world?

Jesus Himself was mightily tempted to exercise authority in some other way than by the power of the Spirit. What was the force of His great temptations at the beginning of His ministry? It is often thought that He was there tempted to doubt whether He was the Messiah. I do not think so. Following hard on the heels of the Baptism, where Jesus' messianic office was confirmed, the force of the temptations was not to cause Him to doubt His mission, but to persuade Him to try to fulfil it by the methods of the world. Each of the three temptations represented one form of the messianic hope among the people of Jesus' day. Had He been willing to follow any one of them, He would have guaranteed for Himself a measure of success, at least for a time. The first was the Mosaic form of the messianic hope. Moses gave manna to his people in the wilderness. If Jesus would be a new Moses, turn stones into bread, and lift the economic burdens from his people's backs, many of them would most certainly have followed Him. And this would have been a worthy work, for their economic needs were great. The second was the Davidic form of the messianic hope. Had not David taken the sword and established his kingdom by might? If Jesus had followed this method, He would at least have had the loyalty of the Zealot party among His people, and could have enjoyed a temporary success until the Romans put down the revolt He led. This, too, was a worthy goal, for His people were languishing under the might of a foreign invader from whom freedom would have been most desirable. The third was the apocalyptic form of the messianic hope. Malachi had suggested that the Lord whom they sought would "suddenly come to his temple" (3:1) to deliver them. There were other apocalyptic visions of a Son of Man making a dramatic appearance on the clouds of heaven to effect a deliverance for His people. Why not, then, make such a dramatic arrival by casting Himself down from the pinnacle of the temple and satisfying His people's hope for a salvation through a marvelous display of heavenly might.

Had Jesus responded to any one of these, He would have had a measure of temporary success, He would have met genuine needs of people, He would have been acceptable to them. But He resisted these. He had come to be the Suffering Servant Messiah, who was here not merely to minister to men's economic, social, and political needs, but to be "wounded for our transgressions," to be "bruised for our iniquities," to heal us with His "stripes," to have the Lord lay "on him the iniquity of us all." He came to be "stricken for the transgression" of His people, to make Himself "an offering for sin," to "make many to be accounted righteous; and . . . bear their iniquities" (Isa. 53:4-11).

Can the church assert her real authority in the world in any way other than by bringing men to the knowledge of this Redeemer? Have we not really lost our theological and spiritual nerve in our time, failing to believe that if we are true to our unique task we shall really make a contribution to the world? What is the nature of the authority Jesus granted to His church? In the parallel passages of Mark 3:15, Matthew 10:1, and Luke 9:1, Jesus granted His disciples authority over "demons" or "unclean spirits," and "diseases," and "every infirmity." This was authority to continue the "signs" of the presence of the messianic kingdom in the messianic community, by which men would be summoned to faith in the Messiah. In Matthew 28:19, 20, the risen Lord indicated that because "I am with you always, to the close of the age," the total "authority in heaven and on earth" which was His would be manifested through the church. But what was the activity through which this authority would be exercised? It was in the commission to "make disciples of all nations, baptizing them in the name of the Father and of the Son and of the Holy Spirit." The exclusive realm of the church's authority here is to evangelize by bringing men of all nations to a knowledge of the triune God. Obviously, this task would have an indirect effect on the whole of life—social, economic, and political. But there seems to be no warrant here for the church to make direct, organized attacks on the established social, economic, and political powers that rule the world; and there seems to be every indication that should such tasks consume the church's energies to the exclusion of bringing men to a saving knowledge of the triune God, the church would be recreant in her peculiar duty to the world. The church is empowered by her Lord to make men know that they belong to God. Karl Barth has commented on this passage: "The task of the apostles, and therefore also of the apostolic Church, consists in baptizing and teaching . . . in the light of Easter morning, in the light of 'the hope laid up for you in heaven' (Col. 1:5)."[46] Add to this the fact that Jesus transferred His "authority on earth to forgive sins" (Mark 2:10) to His church when He gave to it "the keys of the kingdom" whereby "whatever you bind on earth shall be bound in heaven, and whatever you loose on earth shall be loosed in heaven" (Matt. 16:19), and the picture seems to be quite clear. The church's power in the world is spiritual—the power to bear witness to her Lord and through the Holy Spirit lead men to faith in Him. This is a religion of invitation, not of coercion. However much men, even Christian men, must as citizens of this world be involved in all sorts of coercive and repressive social, economic, and political action to restrain the forces of evil which destroy men's lives, the church as church is called to a higher witness and work to be done through the power of the presence of the risen Christ in her midst.

It seems clear that those who advocate the church's direct intervention in the problems of public life are highly selective in the spheres of their advocacy. They argue in many instances that morals cannot be legislated. Therefore, in the areas of sex, pornography, divorce, Sunday "blue laws," abortion, alcoholic beverages, marijuana, and drugs, and in the discipline of students in any realm beyond the academic, the coercive pressures of law should be removed. On the other hand, in matters of race, poverty, war, and ecology, many insist that the church as church should press for binding legislation and take any means of forcing their views on others, even at the expense of the total disruption of the social process and the risk of the total overthrow of the government. There may be a consistency hidden in what seems to be a strange contradiction here, but I find it difficult to see.

Luther and Calvin both had a theocratic idea of society and sought to enforce Christian ideals on the whole nation of which they were a part. They thought of the church as "coextensive with the community, and of a community that should be compulsorily Christian in profession."[47] "In Calvinism," wrote Troeltsch,

> the church is both national and free, a holy community, and an objective institution, a voluntary and a compulsory organization, since it is based upon the assumption that all the elect, if they are sufficiently well taught, will open their minds to the Truth, while it is required that all the non-elect must be suppressed, to the glory of God and for the protection of the elect, and must be prevented from expressing both their unbelief and their non-morality in public.[48]

It was a long and hard struggle to pass on the freedom which the Reformers won from Rome to others who were not Christian at all. Calvin has been much maligned for his efforts to enforce his own understanding of right behavior on all the citizens of his city, and to establish, as nearly as possible, the kingdom of God in Geneva. Cromwell's England has been equally belittled. But those who malign these often seem to emulate them, save that they are highly selective in the areas of social, political, and economic coercion. If those who are opposed to such things as abortion, the relatively uncontrolled use of alcohol, the use of drugs, topless waitresses, prostitution, nude plays, pornographic literature, open dormitory policies on campuses, and the like, should seek to persuade the church as church to enforce these views by legislation and disruption, a loud cry would arise about interference with people's freedom. Would this, however, in principle be highly different from the same approach to questions of war, race, poverty, and ecology?

The church now seems bent on utilizing her strength coercively in public morals but utilizing no coercive power, and often not even her persuasive power, in the realm of private morals. Also, the expenditure of her strength and money in direct assaults on social evil at the expense of her proclamation of the gospel and the teaching of men about the atoning and redeeming act of God in Christ would seem to suggest that, at least subconsciously if not consciously, the church believes that it is possible to produce and maintain the fruits of the Christian faith without that faith. On both counts—that public morality can be maintained without personal morality, and that the social expressions of the Christian faith can be achieved without the faith—the church may be working herself into a cul-de-sac. She is seeking to redeem a culture without demanding that the culture be broken in penitence before the holiness of God.

As long as we leave men "strange to heart-hunger, or soul-despair, or passionate gratitude, or heavenly homesickness . . . Christianity speaks the language of our humane civilization; it does not speak the language of Christ. The age, and much of the Church, believes in civilization and is interested in the Gospel, instead of believing in the Gospel and being interested in civilization."[49] And as long as "we treat as fanatics those who tell us that there is no reconciliation possible between the Cross and culture, when each knows its own mind, except as culture itself submits to be redeemed,"[50] the church is engaged in what may involve a temporary success with culture's blessing, but will in the long run be traitorous to that very culture which it seeks to serve. John Baillie was right in his warnings to men like Gilbert Murray who would openly confess "I am not a Christian," but would then go on to "declare his belief in what he calls 'the precious quality of Christian civilization.' "[51] "To speak thus," said Baillie, "is to cry for the moon."[52] The ultimate basis for the organization of a society is "a belief about *reality,*" and if Christian ideals are to be preserved, how shall this be done without "a Christian belief about reality?"[53]

Those who want "to capture Christian churches and to change them into political and municipal caucuses," said Dale, "compel a serious reconsideration of the true idea of the Church. [They] do not seem to believe in leaven; they want law, and want it swiftly. Nor do they believe in the power of the spirit; they want the letter. They would have had Paul write to Onesimus a letter which would have anticipated Lloyd Garrison, and would have been disappointed by the Apostle's 'want of courage.' "[54] In this regard, the modern church may be repeating the fatal error of the impenitent thief on his cross, who ridiculed One who was more interested in redeeming him from his sin than in ministering to his immediate felt needs, more interested in getting him in right relations with God than in getting him down from that cross where he was "victimized by society." We may be repeating the tragedy of the first Palm Sunday, hailing a king who we hope will solve our outward plight and failing to discover that He has other and more important things to do for us. John Oxenham put it well, and his words are worth serious pondering:

> *They hailed him King as he passed by,*
> *They strewed their garments in the road,*
> *But they were set on earthly things,*
> *And he on God.*

They sang his praise for what he did,
But gave his message little thought;
They could not see that their souls' good
Was all he sought.

They could not understand why he,
With powers so vast at his command,
Should hesitate to claim their rights
And free the land.

Their own concerns and this world's hopes
Shut out the wonder of his news;
And we, with larger knowledge, still
His way refuse.

He walks among us still, unseen,
And still points out the only way,
But we still follow other gods
And him betray.[55]

Whatever else the church does, or does not do, we have failed unless we give people God.

How small, of all that human hearts endure,
That part which kings or laws can cause or cure.[56]

Even if we should solve all the problems of the ghettoes, we would then merely have moved people from that set of problems to the problems of the suburbs. Is that all the church can do for men? I sometimes think that if we could see men's inner lives as God sees them, we might find that the affluent in the suburbs are more torn up inside and have less of a sense of the meaning and purpose of life than many in the ghettoes. Let us, then, be compassionate, considerate, sympathetic to physical, social, mental, and economic needs. Let us minister the love of Christ in ameliorative ways to all men whose lives we touch. Let us be concerned about men's bodies, their minds, their housing, their medical and dental needs, their needs for recreation and fellowship. But let us remember that it is possible that all such needs could be met, and men be no nearer the kingdom of God than before. Let us give men God! There lies the true authority of the church in the world.

To give men God is the most difficult task we can undertake. It may be as slow, as arduous, as demanding as Adoniram Judson's seven years in Burma without a single convert. It may incur the ridicule and even the wrath of the world the church seeks to serve. It may be undramatic and unglamorous. It may involve us, as it did Paul, "in weakness and in much fear and trembling" (I Cor. 2:3). It may make us discover again that the church's impact on the world is not to be measured by size and publicity and approval, that we are not "sufficient of ourselves to claim anything as coming from us," but that "our sufficiency is from God. . . . Therefore, having this ministry by the mercy of God, we do not lose heart" (II Cor. 3:5; 4:1). Who knows the outcome? We may leave that to God.

Vachel Lindsay voiced our hope when he wrote of the "endless line of splendor" spread across the world by the heralds of the Cross, "these troops with heaven for home."

> *What is the final ending?*
> *The issue, can we know?*
> . . . .
>
> *This is our faith tremendous—*
> *Our wild hope, who shall scorn—*
> *That in the name of Jesus,*
> *The world shall be reborn!*[57]

Chapter Six

The Authority of Christ

A Sermon

Text: *The people were astounded at his teaching, for, unlike the doctors of the law, he taught with a note of authority.*

—Mark 1:22, NEB

"Authority" is not a welcome word today. To many, it connotes institutions, structures, organized coercion, raw power. It carries the flavor of curtailment, limitation, repression, restraint. The watchwords today are freedom, participation, independence, autonomy, emancipation, self-determination.

If Jesus were here today, rather than astonishing our generation because "he taught with a note of authority," He would more likely alienate them. The tendency today is to admire Jesus' authority when He can be cited as a backer of a cause in which we are interested, but to forget it when it runs counter to our wills. Some of Jesus' ardent admirers today, having heard that He once drove people out of the Temple, look upon Him with great admiration as a champion of violence, a sort of first-century Che Guevara, a radical proponent of the "theology of revolution." His authority in challenging an institution is lauded. But what about His authority elsewhere? Is He authoritative when He insists on sexual purity? Is He authoritative when He proposes courtesy in dealing with an opponent, or when He advocates meekness, hungering and thirsting after righteousness, chaste speech, a life of prayer, an awareness of the transcendent order of God's world as more real than the things we touch and taste and see?

Some who claim that their ultimate allegiance is to Jesus have even suggested that God is dead. What of Jesus' authority when He insists that God "is not God of the dead but of the living" (Mark 12:27)? A Jewish rabbi once took a God-is-dead theologian to task at this point. He said: "You Christians have been telling us Jews for 2,000 years that there was something of God in this Jesus which we could not see. Now you tell us that the God we were supposed to see does not exist."[1] How can one claim to be loyal to Jesus, without following His authority at the point of His one great certainty—the fact of God?

This suggests that the authority of Jesus is an "authority which men at once resent and crave,"[2] an authority which when it confirms our own views will be welcomed with astonished gladness, as it was by the people described in our text, but which when it runs counter to our own views will be savagely attacked, as it was by Jesus' enemies when in bitter confrontation they hurled at Him the question: "Who gave you authority to act in this way?" (Mark 11:28, NEB). Before the authority of Jesus can have full and final sway, "the world, which is not unready to profess itself enchanted with Christ, must be converted to Him, and subdued, and made . . . another world reconciled and redeemed."[3]

Wherein does the authority of Jesus lie? The only clue in our text is a negative one—it was an authority "unlike the doctors of the law." His authority was a unique kind which made Him stand out from all other teachers of religion in His day. In what did its uniqueness consist?

It hardly consisted in the fact that He was clever and they stupid. The "doctors of the law" in Jesus' day had earned that title by hard study and broad knowledge. They were not charlatans—they were experts. They had a 2,000-year religious tradition of excellence behind them, an excellence which any fair-minded man would have to credit as genuine. One who did battle with these scribes perhaps more than any other—Paul—testified to their superiority when he said: "They are Israelites: they were made God's sons; theirs is the splendour of the divine presence, theirs the covenants, the law, the temple worship, and the promises. Theirs are the patriarchs, and from them, in natural descent, sprang the Messiah. May God, supreme above all, be blessed for ever" for granting to these religious leaders the supreme place of distinction among men of the spirit (Rom. 9:4, 5, NEB). They were men "in undisputed possession of a spiritual supremacy." Jesus, therefore, did not stand out as solitary because He was learned and they inept. He rather stood *with* them at this point, as one rabbi, or teacher, among others. In knowledge of the law He may have matched them, but in this area He was not unique.

Did the authority of Jesus lie, then, in His manner of presenting truth? Would He have been honored by the modern "personality cult"? Were His looks commanding, His gestures effective; was His eye electric, His voice dynamic and appealing, His total demeanor overpowering? Had he been dealing with other subject matter, would He have been an idol of the Hollywood cult? This we do not know, for those who wrote about Him tell us practically nothing about either His physical appearance or His personality. Their almost total indifference to such matters, however, would suggest that they did not rest His authority on them. If His dynamic personal appeal had been fundamental to His power over men, how could they have so consistently refrained from saying so?

Well, then, did His unique authority lie in His subject-matter? When on this occasion the people exclaimed: "A new kind of teaching! He speaks with authority" (Mark 1:27, NEB), or when on another occasion the Temple police remarked: "No man ever spoke as this man speaks" (John 7:46, NEB), were they suggesting that the uniqueness of His teaching lay in the novelty of its content? This is discounted on two grounds. First, the word "new" here does not mean recent, novel, innovative, original, in contrast to something that has been around a long time. It means rather fresh, gripping, inspiring, that which retains or regains its original freshness, such as "a new man" or "a new life," in contrast to that which is wasted, effete, without "vigour, energy, and quickening power." Second, it is now quite well known that Jesus' teachings were not original in content, for practically everything He said was said by some other rabbi. ". . . There is no single moral aphorism recorded as spoken by Jesus," notes one interpreter, "which cannot be paralleled, and often verbally paralleled, in rabbinic literature."[4] The uniqueness of Jesus' authority does not lie in the novelty of the content of His teaching.

Was His authority, then, based on a legal right to command by virtue of His office or His jurisdiction over men? Was He backed by the authority of a kingdom, which enforced its will by magistrate, court, soldier, and steel? He did claim once that He was a king. But what sort of king? He had no throne, no palace, no court, no magistrates, no army, no subjects bound to Him by legal status. And when He was arrested, tried, and condemned by the authority of Rome, He said, "My kingdom does not belong to this world. If it did, my followers would be fighting to save me from arrest" (John 18:36, NEB).

Wherein, then, did the uniqueness of Jesus' authority lie? The conclusion would seem inescapable that His authority lay in His own Person. It was not what He said, nor the manner in which He said it, nor the intellect behind the saying, nor the legal right to speak, which gave His words authority. It was He, Himself, who gave His words authority. The authority was innate to Him. It was simply the effulgence of who He was, the manifestation of the fact that in His own Person He was the inbreaking of God's world into our world. The authority with which He spoke was the authority of God. If there is a God and if by His nature as Creator and Redeemer of men God has inherent authority over men, who are created beings and sinners in need of redemption, then Jesus Christ is authoritative because He bears the authority of God over us. The authority of His words is the authority of His Person.

The "doctors of the law" had no such authority. They neither claimed it, nor desired it, nor impressed those who heard them with having it. Their sole effort was to teach by an authority outside themselves. The scribes "made it their business simply to state, to explain, and to apply the teachings of the Old Testament, together with the decisions of Jewish tribunals, and the sayings of famous teachers in past generations, as handed down by tradition."[5] Their instruction was a "continuous exercise of the memory."[6] Their duty was never to teach anything that they had not been taught. The highest praise that could be given them was that they were "like a well lined with lime, which loses not one drop." They would never say on their own even as much as "Thus saith the Lord." They could only say, "Thus says our tradition."

Jesus not only went beyond them, He even went beyond the writers of the Old Testament whom the scribes were attempting to interpret. Moses could only say to his people, "The Lord, the God of your fathers . . . has sent me to you." The prophets could only say, "The Lord has spoken," or "Thus says the Lord." But Jesus said, rather, "*I* say unto you." He spoke directly, with an inherent authority that was either self-authenticating on the one hand, or on the other hand blasphemy or the raving of a mad man.

On the basis of the entire Gospel presentation of Jesus, it would seem impossible to be enchanted with Him at all unless we accept Him as having "all authority in heaven and on earth" (Matt. 28:18). The only Jesus we know is

the One presented in the Gospels. To pick and choose a
few fragments of that picture and hug them to our breasts
is to create a new and different Jesus of our own fancy
rather than the Jesus of the Gospels. The Gospels confront
us with One who either commands total authority or has
none.

In addition to the open claim of authority for Him,
what else does the Gospel portrait offer us? It shows us
one who was bold enough to deepen, and even to correct,
the Old Testament law, which was considered to have been
directly given by God. He claims that He has come to fulfil
the law. He sets down the requirements for entering the
kingdom of heaven. He lays down the basis on which men
shall see God. He forgives sin. He claims to be the final
Judge and insists that men's standing in the last judgment
will depend on their relationship to Him. He boldly calls to
men: "Come to me, all who labor and are heavy-laden, and
I will give you rest" (Matt. 11:28). He calls on men to give
Him an absolute loyalty transcending all other highest
loyalties, such as loyalty to parents and spouse. He dares
to say to a dying thief, on His own authority, "Today you
will be with me in Paradise" (Luke 23:43).

But it is not only His sayings that have this "ring of
authority"; His words do also. In the passage we are
considering, the impression of His authority was deepened
by the fact that with a word of command He cast out an
"unclean spirit" from a poor, deranged man. The people
"were all dumbfounded" and said to one another, "When
he gives orders, even the unclean spirits submit" (Mark
1:27, NEB). The Jews of Jesus' day were familiar with
exorcisms of evil spirits, but these were done through
magical formulae, accompanied by supernatural signs such
as shattering a statue or overturning a bowl or drawing the
demon from the nose of the possessed by means of a ring.
They were not done by the power of a direct command.
Here men saw Jesus' word of power authoritative even
over "the uncontrollable wills of spirits who defied all

moral obligations." Both in word and deed, then, Jesus, although identifying Himself with us as men, put Himself over on God's side of the divine-human relationship. He was man as are we, but there was never other man like Him. If He were mere man, His religious sensibilities would have directed men away from Himself to God. On the contrary, however, He concentrates "upon Himself the consideration, the devotion, the love, which should be given to God only. . . . He points us straight to Himself, as the unique and supreme and unchanging object of man's regard."[7]

We cannot dismiss this as a misinterpretation of Jesus by the Gospel writers, or ignore it on the ground that the early church attributed to Him a character other than He really had. For one thing, how could we know this, for we know nothing of Him save what they tell us? Furthermore, if the impression He made on them was so drastically out of accord with what He actually was, then He failed miserably as a monotheistic Jew even to keep fellow-Jews from a new idolatry in deifying Him. Could we admire or follow a man who so tragically failed at this point?

No, to raise the question of Jesus' authority is to raise the old, yet ever new question: "Whom say ye that I am?" His authority and His Person cannot finally be kept separate. We must take Him for what the Gospels claim Him to be; or dismiss Him as a pathetically deranged religious enthusiast to be pitied; or a bold, proud, insufferable blasphemer, to be rejected.

The Gospel of Mark from which our passage comes introduces the whole story by calling it "the gospel of Jesus Christ, the Son of God." This does not mean merely the good news which He brought in His teaching. It means the good news about *Him*, the good news inherent in who He was, in His life, death, resurrection, ascension, and present Lordship over the universe.

If His word has the authority of God because He *was* God, He commands us totally, soul and body, through His inherent right to exercise authority over us. We gladly accept that authority, which we acknowledge as legitimate because it is divine. We gladly respond to the self-authentication of His claims in His Person, and bow before Him, saying: "My Lord and my God." If Jesus was what He claimed to be, then we are "awed and subdued before the grace and grandeur of a moral superior . . . not because he *suggests,* but because he *realises,* a higher conception of excellence"[8] which puts Him in the place of God to us. If, on the other hand, He was not what He is claimed to have been, then He is a mere ideal of the imagination which "is simply added to my culture, but does not transform my life."[9]

Where do we stand with regard to this issue? Do we join with the apostolic church which obviously accepted the "note of authority" in Jesus' teaching and deeds as the authority of God? Or do we stand with His enemies, who hurled at Him the question: "Who gave you authority to act in this way"?

We are free to choose. But a choice against Him says more about us than it does about Him. The late Dr. H. Scott Holland of the Anglican Church makes a statement that ought to be repeated here. He insists that "the cleavage" between those who accept Christ's authority and those who do not "is moral, due to the antecedent ethical condition of the man, before the coming of the Lord. The coming forces a decision, and the decision springs out of the character the man brings with Him. It is therefore a Revelation, a Judgment."[10]

Why is this? Because the only way to apprehend Jesus' authority over us is by faith. And what is a life of faith? It is one that draws its life from elsewhere, has no life in itself, no virtue of its own, lays itself in another's hands and will, finds the force of its existence outside itself. Karl Barth has said, "Faith is the abdication of vain-glorious man from his vain-glory."[11] This is exactly what the Sonship of Jesus was. It was a selflessness, a total dependence on God, a deriving of life from Him to the point that He could say, "the Son can do nothing by himself; he does only what he sees the Father doing" (John 5:19, NEB). This means that He was never independent of God, that He never made His own will the rival of God's will, as the first Adam did, but always lived in dependence on Him, thus fulfilling God's intention in creating man by finding His perfect freedom in perfect obedience. So, says Scott Holland, the true Sonship of Jesus can be detected only by a "moral temperamental sympathy" with Him. "The pressure of the Blessed Presence forces the will to disclose its secret choice,"[12] whether we are with Him or against Him.

Where do we stand? What is our "secret choice"? Let none of us try to escape the judgment which His claim to authority over us involves. We are free to reject, but that rejection merely indicates a moral disposition to love darkness rather than light. It says that we do not really believe in God, or we would respond to the God in Him. Our problem is not, as we so often think, intellectual. It is not that we have insufficient evidence. It is not that critical study has shattered the records of Jesus' life and done away with a firm basis on which to believe on Him. P. T. Forsyth reminds us that "Belief rests not merely on evidence but on the will to believe."[13] Whatever critical study and modern thought have to say, we have the picture of Jesus given us in the Gospels, and we cannot escape that. There was never such a One pictured elsewhere. He stands before us solitary and alone. He claims final authority over us—in values, in decisions, in actions, in life, in death, at the final judgment.

Notes

CHAPTER I

1 *Grace Abounding to the Chief of Sinners* (London: Hodder and Stoughton, 1888), pp. 123f.

2 *Creeds and Critics* (London: A. R. Mowbray, 1918), p. 88.

3 J. N. Sanders, *The Foundations of the Christian Faith* (New York: Philosophical Library, 1952), p. 184.

4 *History of the English People* (Chicago: Belford, Clarke, 1882), III, 14.

5 *The Way, The Truth, The Life* (London: Macmillan, 1897), p. 177.

6 *Positive Preaching and the Modern Mind* (Cincinnati: Jennings & Graham, 1907), pp. 286f.

7 R. H. Murray, *Erasmus & Luther* (London: Society for Promoting Christian Knowledge, 1920), p. 213.

8 George W. Richards, *Christian Ways of Salvation* (New York: Macmillan, 1923), p. 237.

9 Georges Lefebvre, *The Coming of the French Revolution* (New York: Random House, 1957), p. xv.

10 *Selected Writings of Martin Luther, 1517-1520,* ed. Theodore G. Tappert (Philadelphia: Fortress Press, 1967), p. 336.

11 Emil Brunner, *Christianity and Civilization* (London: Nisbet, 1948), I, 132.

12 *Ibid.,* p. 123.

13 Quoted by Brunner, *ibid.*

14 Definition of "equality" in *The Century Dictionary and Cyclopedia* (New York: Century, 1901).

15 *Christianity and Civilization,* p. 138.

16 Act I, scene 3.

17 Reinhold Niebuhr, *The Nature and Destiny of Man* (New York: Scribner's, 1943), II, 206.

18 George W. Richards, *Beyond Fundamentalism and Modernism* (New York: Scribner's, 1934), pp. 247f.

19 Trans. Donald Atwater (London: Sheed and Ward, 1933), pp. 54-56.

20 Brunner, *Christianity and Civilization,* p. 132.

[21] *Nature, Man and God* (London: Macmillan, 1934), p. 20.

[22] *Ibid.,* pp. 20f.

[23] *Studies in Theology* (London: Hodder and Stoughton, 1895), pp. 221f.

[24] *Nature, Man and God,* pp. 348f.

[25] *The Works of President Edwards* (New York: Leavitt & Allen, 1856), I, 7.

[26] Gerhard Ebeling, *Luther,* trans. R. A. Wilson (Philadelphia: Fortress Press, 1964), p. 92.

[27] Quoted by T. A. Kantonen, "Protestantism in Education," *The Christian Century,* November 12, 1947.

[28] C. J. Cadoux, article in the *Christian World,* April 27, 1944, quoted by E. C. Blackman, *Biblical Interpretation* (Philadelphia: Westminster, 1957), pp. 52f.

[29] *The Principle of Authority in Relation to Certainty, Sanctity and Society,* 2nd ed. (London: Independent Press, 1952), p. 295.

[30] *Selected Writings, 1517-1520,* p. 209.

[31] Quoted by Gerhard Ebeling, *Luther,* p. 229.

[32] Quoted by H. Scott Holland, *Creeds and Critics,* pp. 209f.

[33] *Confessions,* VI, xx.

[34] *Selected Writings of Martin Luther, 1520-1523,* ed. Theodore G. Tappert (Philadelphia: Fortress Press, 1967), p. 229.

[35] *Selected Writings of Martin Luther, 1529-1546,* ed. Theodore G. Tappert (Philadelphia: Fortress Press, 1967), p. 373.

[36] Quoted by Ebeling, *Luther,* p. 40.

CHAPTER II

[1] *The Servant of the Word* (New York: Scribner's, 1942), pp. 18f.

[2] *Evangelical Theology* (London: William Collins, 1965, Fontana Books), p. 34.

[3] *Werke* (Weimar: Böhlan, 1892), V, 23.

[4] *Creeds and Critics,* p. 187.

[5] Quoted by Luther, *Selected Writings of Martin Luther, 1529-1546,* p. 243.

[6] *Ibid.,* p. 217.

[7] *Ibid.,* p. 218.

[8] *Selected Writings, 1517-1520,* pp. 6, 8.

[9] *Studies in Theology,* p. 226.

[10] Frederick W. Schroeder, *Preaching the Word with Authority* (Philadelphia: Westminster, 1954), p. 117.

[11] *Selected Writings, 1529-1546,* p. 376.

[12] Quoted by George W. Richards, *Beyond Fundamentalism and Modernism* (New York: Scribner's, 1934), p. 168.

13 *Selected Writings, 1523-1526,* pp. 50f.

14 *Ibid.,* p. 56.

15 *Ibid.,* p. 58.

16 *The Flower of Grass* (New York: Harper, 1945), p. 94.

17 Wolf-Dieter Zimmermann, "Finkenwalde," in *I Knew Dietrich Bonhoeffer,* eds. Wolf-Dieter Zimmermann and Ronald Gregor Smith, trans. Käthe Gregor Smith (New York: Harper, 1966), p. 107.

18 *Ibid.*

19 *Positive Preaching and the Modern Mind,* p. 288.

20 *Beyond Fundamentalism and Modernism,* p. 178.

21 *Biblical Interpretation,* p. 49.

22 Francis Thompson, "The Kingdom of God."

23 *Positive Preaching and the Modern Mind,* p. 277.

24 *Creeds and Critics,* pp. 107ff.

25 *Ibid.,* p. 112.

26 *Positive Preaching and the Modern Mind,* pp. 278ff.

27 *Ibid.,* pp. 282f.

28 Quoted by F. W. Farrar, *The Bible, Its Meaning and Supremacy* (New York: Longmans, Green, 1899), p. 278.

CHAPTER III

1 *Creeds and Critics,* p. 205.

2 *Ibid.,* pp. 205f.

3 *Selected Writings, 1529-1546,* pp. 375f.

4 *Creeds and Critics,* pp. 206f.

5 *Vision and Authority* (London: Hodder and Stoughton, 1928), pp. 99ff.

6 *Studies in Theology,* p. 209.

7 See Donald G. Miller, *Fire in Thy Mouth* (New York and Nashville: Abingdon, 1954), pp. 42ff.

8 *The Riddle of the New Testament* (New York: Harcourt, Brace, 1931), pp. 252f.

9 *Ibid.,* p. 160.

10 *Selected Writings, 1529-1546,* pp. 375f.

11 *The Significance of the Bible for the Church,* trans. Carl Rasmussen (Philadelphia: Fortress Press, 1963), p. 29.

12 (New York: Scribner's, 1967), p. 63.

13 *Ibid.,* p. 107.

14 *Ibid.,* p. 108.

15 *The Church's One Foundation* (London: Hodder and Stoughton, 1908), p. 110.

16 Quoted by John H. Rodgers, *The Theology of P. T. Forsyth* (London: Independent Press, 1965), p. 159.

17 *Ibid.*, p. 162.

18 Quoted by Nygren, *The Significance of the Bible for the Church*, p. 13.

19 P. T. Forsyth, *Religion in Recent Art* (London: Hodder and Stoughton, 1901), p. ix.

20 *Christian Letters to a Post-Christian World* (Grand Rapids: Eerdmans, 1969), p. 169.

21 *Ibid.*, p. 168.

22 *Religion in Recent Art*, p. ix.

23 Quoted by Nygren, *The Significance of the Bible for the Church*, pp. 18f. (I am deeply indebted to Nygren for the trend of the argument here.)

24 *Ibid.*, pp. 18-19, 27.

CHAPTER IV

1 Quoted by W. E. Garrison in a review of *Great Books of the Western World*, ed. Robert Maynard Hutchins and Mortimer J. Adler, in *The Christian Century*, October 1, 1952.

2 Grand Rapids: Eerdmans, 1971, pp. 85f.

3 Nehemiah Curnock, ed., standard edition (London: Charles H. Kelly, 1909), II, 226.

4 *The Significance of the Bible for the Church*, pp. 38f.

5 P. T. Forsyth, *The Work of Christ*, second edition (London: Independent Press, 1958), p. 41.

6 *Creeds and Critics*, p. 101.

7 *Ibid.*

8 F. W. H. Myers, *Saint Paul* (London: Macmillan, 1935), p. 44.

9 Gerhard Ebeling, *Luther*, p. 40.

10 See *Selected Writings of Martin Luther, 1520-1523*, p. 226.

11 *Ibid.*

12 *Ibid.*, p. 227.

13 *Ibid.*

14 *Ibid.*, pp. 227f.

15 See P. T. Forsyth, *The Principle of Authority*, p. 188.

16 *Ibid.*, p. 70.

17 *Ibid.*, p. 181.

18 *Christian Missions and the Judgment of God* (London: SCM Press, 1953), p. 16.

19 *The Significance of the Bible for the Church*, p. 39.

20 "Guiding Principles for the Interpretation of the Bible," *Interpretation*, October, 1949, pp. 457ff.

21 *The Forgiveness of Sins* (London: Macmillan, 1916), pp. 177f.

22 *Positive Preaching and the Modern Mind*, p. 192.

23 Quoted by John Baillie, *A Diary of Readings* (New York: Scribner's, 1955), Day 151.

[24] *Ibid.*, Day 115.

[25] *Ibid.*

[26] *Preaching the Word with Authority* (Philadelphia: Westminster, 1954), p. 113.

[27] Quoted by Roy A. Harrisville, *His Hidden Grace* (New York: Abingdon, 1965), p. 81.

[28] Quoted by T. R. Glover, *The Jesus of History* (London: SCM Press, 1918), p. 61.

[29] *Creeds and Critics*, p. 109.

[30] *The Principle of Authority*, p. 75.

[31] Review of John Oman's *Vision and Authority* in *The British Weekly*, December 20, 1928.

[32] *The French Revolution: A History* (New York: Harper, 1873), I, 50.

[33] *Creeds and Critics*, pp. 201f.

CHAPTER V

[1] *The Good News According to Mark* (Richmond: John Knox, 1970), p. 251.
    Since writing the above I have come across a significant confirmatory statement by Karl Adam. He writes: "The human value is not the ultimate, but only the penultimate value; the last, the highest value is God the Father. . . . Because this Father loves men . . . are we to love men. My relation to men has therefore its ultimate roots in a transcendental fact, namely in that fundamental relation of love in which God includes men, all men. . . . That is the reason why man is worth loving: not by reason of what he is in himself or for himself, but by reason of what he is for God, or in the language of theology: not for a natural but for a supernatural reason. I shall never reach man by starting from the earth; I must first reach to heaven to find man through God. The floodstream of the love of man passes through the heart of God. I must first have God before I can have man. God is the way to man. . . . No one has expressed this truth with greater profundity than the apostle of love, St. John: 'Everyone that loveth is born to God and knoweth God.' " — *Two Essays*, English translation (New York: Macmillan, 1930), pp. 61-66.

[2] Christopher Dawson, *The Making of Europe* (New York: World, 1956, Meridian Books), p. xix.

[3] *Studies in Theology*, p. 201.

[4] Andrew Marvel, "To His Coy Mistress."

[5] *What Is Christian Civilization?* (London: Oxford, 1945), p. 50.

[6] *Ibid.*

[7] *Ibid.*, p. 56.

[8] Quoted by John H. Rodgers, *The Theology of P. T. Forsyth*, p. 23.

[9] *The Cruciality of the Cross* (London: Hodder and Stoughton, 1910), pp. 39f.; pp. 31f.

[10] *Ibid.*, pp. 32f.

11 A. W. W. Dale, *The Life of R. W. Dale of Birmingham* (London: Hodder and Stoughton, 1898), p. 670.

12 *Ibid.*, p. 676.

13 *Ibid.*, p. 585.

14 *Ibid.*, p. 587.

15 *Ibid.*, p. 648.

16 *Ibid.*, pp. 649f.

17 (New York: Dutton, 1943, Everyman's Library), pp. 9f.

18 Reinhold Niebuhr, *The Nature and Destiny of Man*, II, 152.

19 *The Christian Century*, January 22, 1969, p. 107.

20 *The Kingdom and the Power* (Philadelphia: Westminster, 1950), pp. 242-44. See also my own chapter on "God Reconciles and Makes Free," in *Reconciliation in Today's World*, ed. Allen O. Miller (Grand Rapids: Eerdmans, 1969), pp. 27ff.

21 *Biblical Theology in Crisis* (Philadelphia: Westminster, 1970), p. 94.

22 *Ibid.*, p. 101.

23 Edwin Lewis, *The Practice of the Christian Life* (Philadelphia: Westminster, 1942), pp. 18, 22.

24 This comes from an oral report by a close friend of Dr. Hromadka.

25 John H. Rodgers, *The Theology of P. T. Forsyth*, p. 19.

26 *The Justification of God* (London: Latimer House Limited, 1948), p. 116.

27 P. T. Forsyth, quoted by John H. Rodgers, *The Theology of P. T. Forsyth*, p. 72.

28 P. T. Forsyth, *Positive Preaching and the Modern Mind*, p. 122. Dorothy Sayers has a trenchant passage which is instructive at this point: "The chief danger is lest the Churches, having for so long acquiesced in the exploiting of the many by the few, should now think to adjust the balance by helping on the exploitation of the few by the many, instead of attacking the false standards by which everybody, rich and poor alike, has now come to assess the value of life and work. If the Churches make this mistake, they will again be merely following the shift of power from one class of the community to the other and deserting the dying Caesar to enlist the support of his successor." *Christian Letters to a Post-Christian World* (Grand Rapids: Eerdmans, 1969), p. 136.

28a *Studies in Theology*, p. 201.

29 *Positive Preaching and the Modern Mind*, pp. 195f.

30 *Ibid.*, p. 123.

31 *The Life of R. W. Dale of Birmingham*, p. 670.

32 *Ibid.*, pp. 648f.

33 *Wesley as Sociologist, Theologian, Churchman* (New York: The Methodist Book Concern, 1918), pp. 7f.

34 *Ibid.*, pp. 32f.

35 *Ibid.*, p. 33.

36 *A History of England in the 18th Century* (New York: Appleton, 1883), II, 691f.

37 *The Life of R. W. Dale of Birmingham*, p. 649.

38 Peyton H. Hoge, *Moses Drury Hoge: Life and Letters* (Richmond, Virginia: Presbyterian Committee of Publication, 1899), p. 203.

39 *Ibid.*, p. 204.

40 *Ibid.*, pp. 204f.

41 *Ibid.*, p. 205.

42 *Ibid.*, p. 206.

43 *Ibid.*

44 *Ibid.*, pp. 206f.

45 *Ibid.*, pp. 207f.

46 "An Exegetical Study of Matthew 28:16-20," in *The Theology of the Christian Mission*, ed. Gerald H. Anderson (New York: McGraw-Hill, 1961), pp. 69f.

47 John Baillie, *What Is Christian Civilization?*, p. 14.

48 *The Social Teaching of the Christian Churches*, trans. Olive Wyon (New York: Macmillan, 1931), II, 653.

49 P. T. Forsyth, *Positive Preaching and the Modern Mind*, p. 194.

50 *Ibid.*

51 *What Is Christian Civilization?*, p. 47.

52 *Ibid.*, p. 49.

53 *Ibid.*

54 *The Life of R. W. Dale of Birmingham*, pp. 649f.

55 "He—They—We."

56 Samuel Johnson, "Lines Added to Goldsmith's Traveller."

57 "Foreign Missions in Battle Array."

CHAPTER VI

1 In a discussion at Pittsburgh Theological Seminary.

2 P. T. Forsyth, *Positive Preaching and the Modern Mind*, p. 119.

3 *Ibid.*, p. 131.

4 Edwyn Hoskyns and Noel Davey, *The Riddle of the New Testament* (London: Faber and Faber, 1958), p. 135.

5 John A. Broadus, *Commentary on the Gospel of Matthew* (Philadelphia: American Baptist Publication Society, 1886), p. 172.

6 Emil Schürer, *The Jewish People in the Time of Jesus Christ* (Edinburgh: T. & T. Clark, 1885), II, 1, 324.

7 Scott Holland, *Creeds and Critics*, p. 99.

8 See W. Robertson Nicoll, *The Church's One Foundation* (London: Hodder & Stoughton, 1908), pp. 202f.

9 *Ibid.*

10 *The Fourth Gospel* (London: John Murray, 1923), p. 151.

11 *Church Dogmatics* (Edinburgh: T. & T. Clark, 1956), IV/1/618.

12 *The Fourth Gospel,* p. 87.

13 Quoted by John H. Rodgers, *The Theology of P. T. Forsyth,* pp. 218f.